KEYBOARD SHORTCUTS	COMMAND OR ACTION
Shift-Command-H	Formula Find Previous command
Command-f	Data Find Next command
Shift-Command-F	Data Find Previous command
Command-e	Data Extract command
Command-=	Options Calculate Now command
Command-a	Chart Select Chart command
Command-m	Activate next window
Command-Shift-M	Activate previous window
Command-.	Cancel
Command-w	Close command (active window)
Command-'	Copy the formula from the cell above into the formula bar
Command-Enter	Enter an array formula
Option-Enter	Fill a selection with a formula
Command-Hyphen	Insert the date into the formula bar
Command-;	Insert the time into the formula bar
Command-a	Select all cells

The SYBEX Prompter Series

EXCEL INSTANT REFERENCE

The SYBEX Prompter Series

We've designed the SYBEX Prompter Series to meet the evolving needs of software users, who want essential information presented in an accessible format. Our best authors have distilled their expertise into compact *Instant Reference* books you can use to look up the precise use of any command—its syntax, available options, and operation. More than just summaries, these books also provide realistic examples and insights into effective usage drawn from our authors' wealth of experience.

The SYBEX Prompter Series also includes these titles:

Lotus 1-2-3 Instant Reference
Greg Harvey and Kay Yarborough Nelson

WordPerfect Instant Reference
Greg Harvey and Kay Yarborough Nelson

WordPerfect 5 Instant Reference
Greg Harvey and Kay Yarborough Nelson

dBASE Instant Reference
Alan Simpson

Turbo BASIC Instant Reference
Douglas Hergert

DOS Instant Reference
Greg Harvey and Kay Yarborough Nelson

HyperTalk Instant Reference
Greg Harvey

WordStar Instant Reference
David J. Clark

Ventura Instant Reference
Matthew Holtz

Hard Disk Instant Reference
Judd Robbins

The SYBEX Prompter™ Series

EXCEL INSTANT REFERENCE

William J. Orvis

San Francisco • Paris • Düsseldorf • London

The SYBEX Prompter Series
Editor in Chief: Rudolph S. Langer
Managing Editor: Barbara Gordon
Series Editor: James A. Compton
Copy Editor: Michael L. Wolk

Cover design by Thomas Ingalls + Associates
Series design by Ingrid Owen

Library of Congress Card Number: **88-80005**
ISBN **0-89588-577-8**
Manufactured in the United States of America
10 9 8 7 6 5 4 3 2 1

DEDICATION

This book is dedicated to Holt International Children's Services, an organization with the simple goal of bringing together children who need parents and parents who need children, and to the son they are bringing us.

ACKNOWLEDGMENTS

This book is the result of a project to compress all of the functionality of Microsoft Excel into the compact format of a SYBEX *Instant Reference.* I initially thought "no problem," and then delivered enough text for a book twice the intended size. The series editor, Jim Compton, and I chopped at the text, modified the format, and tucked things in here and there to make it all fit. We were constantly faced with the pain of having to decide whether to remove something to make room for just one more important fact.

Of course, everybody at home wanted to help, especially my one-year old daughter. She loves to type on Daddy's computer, usually when he is not looking. For a while there I thought my machine was going bad—whole pages would disappear and be replaced with meaningless text. Then I caught my little helper typing away, having a great time. That's when I showed her how the Caps Lock key makes a little red light turn on, and having her play with that kept both of us happy.

I want to thank Jim Compton for his efforts and Dianne King and Rudy Langer for suggesting the topic. Thanks also to Barbara Gordon, managing editor; Michael L. Wolk, copy editor; Dan Tauber, technical reviewer; Bob Myren, word processor; Charles Cowens, desktop publishing specialist; Ami Knox, proofreader; Suzanne Albertson, book designer and paste-up artist; Sonja Schenk, graphics technician; Ingrid Owen, series designer, and Jonathan Rinzler, production coordinator.

I also want to thank Julie, my wife, for keeping the kids off my back so I could get some work done. Finally, thanks to my three (soon to be four) little helpers, Sierra, Skye, and B.J.

William J. Orvis
Livermore, California

Table of Contents

INTRODUCTION

The *Excel Instant Reference* is designed to give users quick and easy access to descriptions of the commands, functions (including macro functions) and options of Microsoft Excel on the Macintosh through Version 1.5.

Audience

The *Excel Instant Reference* is designed for the knowledgeable user of Excel. It is not a tutorial for beginners. There are a number of good tutorials available (*Mastering Excel on the Macintosh*, by Carl Townsend, SYBEX, 1988, for example). Once you know the basics of Microsoft Excel, this book will be an invaluable tool for your everyday use of the program. Especially for the worksheet and macro functions, the short, concise descriptions given here are generally all that is required to help you apply Excel to your work.

Organization

This book has two main parts. Part 1, Menu Commands and Macro Functions, alphabetically presents Excel's macro functions and their equivalent menu commands. At the beginning is a table cross-referencing the menu commands with the associated macro functions. To learn the operation of a command, find it in the table, and then look up the referenced macro function. Menu commands without macro equivalents are grouped together before the functions. Note that the macro functions can be used only on a macro sheet.

Part 2, Operators and Worksheet Functions, presents Excel's operators and worksheet functions. While the macros perform the command and control functions, the operators and worksheet functions perform the data manipulation. The worksheet functions can be used on worksheets and macro sheets.

In addition, this Introduction contains the basic conventions used in Excel and this book. It also contains descriptions of the basic data structures used in Excel, such as integers and numbers, strings, arrays and the database, and information about directory paths and navigating dialog boxes.

Inside the front and back covers are lists of the keyboard shortcuts and the ASCII codes and printable characters for the Geneva font.

Conventions

The conventions used in this book are straightforward. A formula is a mathematical or string equation that you type into a cell, and that shows in the formula bar when the cell is selected. A formula expresses, in Excel's notation, an equation you want the program to calculate. Formulas also consist of constants such as numbers and strings that you type directly into a cell.

The *value* of a cell is what you see in a cell on the worksheet. It is the result of the formula in the cell. For constants, the formula and the value will be the same.

In the function descriptions, variable arguments appear in italic type, enclosed by angle brackets (*<name>*). Optional variables are also enclosed in square brackets ([*<optional_name>*]). Alternate arguments are surrounded with square brackets and separated with vertical bars ([*<option_a>* | *<option_b>*]). Characters typed by the user appear in boldface type.

When two keystrokes appear in text joined by a hyphen (for example, *Command-A*), you should press the first key and hold it down while you press the second one. When two keystrokes are separated by a space (for example, *Command-A*), you should press and release the first key before pressing the second.

The notation V:*n* in entry headings indicates the numbered release of Excel in which the command or function first became available.

Contents of Cells

The cells in an Excel worksheet can contain arrays, formulas, or any of five types of data values. The following paragraphs discuss each of these entities, beginning with data types.

Types of Data Values

Excel has five types of values you can calculate with: numbers, strings, logical values, dates, and times. Real or decimal numbers are numeric values in the range 2.225×10^{-308} to $1.798 \times 10^{+308}$, with up to 14 digits of precision. Strings are lists of up to 255 alphanumeric characters. The logical values are TRUE and FALSE. Dates and times are stored as numbers representing days and fractional parts of days counting from January 1, 1904. Excel also uses integers, which are numbers with no fractional part, and arrays, which are rectangular groups of values.

Three types of values have a special effect on a cell; dates, times, and percents. If you type a date or time into a cell in one of Excel's date and time formats (see the **Format Number** command), Excel will automatically convert it into a *serial day number.* A date is represented with a *serial day number* as the number of days between that date and January 1, 1904 The time is included in a *serial day number* as a fractional part of a day. Excel will then format the cell as a date or time, so that it appears to contain the date or time as text. However, the value of the cell is the *serial day number.*

Percents are handled in a similar manner. If you enter a number postfixed with a percent symbol (%) into a cell, Excel will divide that number by 100 and then format the cell as percent. Thus you will still see the percent as you typed it, but the value of the cell will be 1/100 that value.

If you type dates, times or percents in formulas, the same conversions will be made, but the cell will not be automatically formatted. If you want a special format in a cell containing a formula, use the Format Number command.

Error Values Whenever Excel encounters an error in a calculation, it will return an error value to the cell containing the error. The error values appear as the text strings shown in Table I.1. Error values will propagate through the worksheet, until all cells that depend on the erroneous cell also show an error value. In this way, all bad values, and any calculations that depend on those values, will be marked as erroneous. You can trap error values with the IF() function and the IS*x*() functions.

Formulas

Formulas are where the real power of a spreadsheet lies, because they are where you can combine the values to produce new information, or to extract information that was not evident from the initial values. The formulas in Excel perform the calculations on the worksheet, and formulas are combinations of values, operators and functions.

ERROR VALUE	CAUSE
#DIV/0!	Division by zero
#NAME?	A variable name in a formula has not been defined.
#N/A	A value is not available, or the NA() function has been used.
#NULL!	A result has no value.
#NUM!	Numeric overflow, underflow, or incorrect use of a number (for example, SQRT(–1)).
#REF!	Invalid cell reference; the cell either is not on the worksheet or has been deleted.
#VALUE!	Invalid argument type (for example, text where a number is required).

Table I.1: Excel error values

Every formula in Excel, except for constant values, starts with an equal sign (=), which tells Excel to treat the contents of a cell as a formula, and to attempt to interpret it and calculate its value. Cells without the initial equal sign are treated as numbers, logical values, dates, or text, depending on the contents. Excel will first check the first character of a cell to see if it contains a formula. If the first character is not an equal sign, Excel will try to interpret the contents of a cell as a number, then a logical value, and then a date. It assumes everything else to be a string.

Arrays and Vectors

In Excel, you can also work with arrays, which are made up of numbers, strings, logical values, dates, and times. An array is a one- or two-dimensional arrangement of values or cells.

$$\begin{vmatrix} 1 & 2 & 3 \\ 4 & 5 & 6 \\ 7 & 8 & 9 \end{vmatrix} \qquad \begin{vmatrix} \text{"one"} & \text{"two"} & \text{"three"} \end{vmatrix} \qquad \begin{vmatrix} 183.6 \\ 272.8 \\ 27.4 \end{vmatrix}$$

For example, three possible arrays are

The first example is a three-by-three array of numbers, the second is a one-by-three array of strings, and the third is a three-by-one array of numbers. The last two examples are also known as horizontal and vertical vectors, respectively.

An array located in the cells of a worksheet is described with a standard cell reference. For example, if the first array above was located in rows 1, 2, and 3 and columns A, B, and C, it would be referenced as A1:C3. If an array is to be explicitly written out, it is written between braces ({ }), with consecutive cells on a row separated with commas, and rows separated with semicolons. The first example would be written {1,2,3;4,5,6;7,8,9}.

Output Arrays Some functions return an array as a result, which cannot be stored in a single cell. If you enter them into one cell, you will only see the value in the upper-left corner of the array. To enter these functions and see all of the array values, select an appropriately sized array of cells, type the function into the first element of this selection, and press Enter or click on the check box while holding down the Command key. The function will then be entered into all of the selected cells as an output array. If you look at the contents of one of the cells in an output array, you will notice that it contains the original formula, surrounded by braces. This is Excel's way of marking these cells as part of an array. Do not type these braces yourself.

Array Formulas Operators and functions that operate on single values can be made to operate on arrays of values. To do this, select a set of cells for the output that is the same size as the input array. Type the formula into the upper-left cell of the selected range, inserting array references or arrays where the single values normally would go. Hold down the Command key when pressing Enter or clicking in the check box. The formula will be entered into all of the cells as an array, with braces surrounding the formula. When the formula is evaluated, values from the equivalent positions in the input arrays will be inserted into the formula, and the results will be placed in the equivalent position in the output selection. For example, **{1,2;3,4}+{5,6;7,8}** will return the array {1+5,2+6;3+7,4+8} or {6,8;10,12}.

If any input array is incomplete, Excel will attempt to expand it to the same size as the others by repeating values. For example, if a vertical vector is used where a square array is needed, the values in each row of the vector will be repeated into the rest of the cells in that row. The formula **1+{2,3;4,5}** would be expanded to {1,1;1,1}+{2,3;4,5}, and the formula **{1;2}*{3,4;5,6}** would be expanded to {1,1;2,2}*{3,4;5,6}. If Excel cannot logically expand an array, it will return the error value #N/A.

Table I.2 lists the functions that cannot be used in array formulas, because they either have no arguments, require arrays for all of their arguments, or give arrays as results.

Arrays are extremely powerful worksheet constructs. Learning to use them will almost always be to your benefit.

AND()	LINEST()	ROW()
AREAS()	LOGEST()	ROWS()
AVERAGE()	MAX()	STDEV()
CELL()	MDETERM()	STDEVP()
COLUMN()	MIN()	SUM()
COLUMNS()	MINVERSE()	T()
COUNT()	MMULT()	TRANSPOSE()
COUNTA()	N()	TREND()
FALSE()	NA()	TRUE()
GROWTH()	NOW()	VAR()
INDEX()	OR()	VARP()
INDIRECT()	PI()	
ISREF()	RAND()	

Table I.2: Functions that cannot be used in array formulas

Cell Referencing

Two cell referencing styles are available in Excel: A1 and R1C1. The A1 style is similar to that used in VisiCalc and Lotus 123; it is the default style used in Excel. In the A1 style, the letter refers to the column and the number refers to the row. The R1C1 style of cell referencing is used in Microsoft Multiplan, and can be used by executing the Options R1C1 command. In the R1C1 style, the R stands for row, the C stands for column, and the numbers indicate which row and column. While you can switch between the A1 and R1C1 styles of referencing for most normal references, if a reference is required for an argument of a function as a string, it must be a string in the R1C1 style. Also, if a function returns a reference as a string, it will be in the R1C1 style.

Besides differing in the style in which they are entered, cell references in Excel are also classified as either absolute or relative. *Absolute* cell references refer to a particular cell on the worksheet. If the contents of a cell is copied to another cell, absolute cell references do not change. In the A1 style, an absolute cell reference is created by placing a dollar sign before the part of a cell reference that you want to lock. For example, B5 refers to cell B5, and will not change if the reference is moved to another cell. In the R1C1 style, an absolute cell reference is written as R5C2, which would also refer to cell B5 on the worksheet.

A relative cell reference is adjustable, pointing to a cell that is at a relative position to the cell containing the reference. For example, if the reference B5 is in a formula in cell C4, the reference does not refer to the absolute cell B5, but to the cell that is one row down and one column to the left of cell C4. If the formula in cell C4 is copied to cell D5, the reference will change from B5 to C6. In the R1C1 style, this is written as R[1]C[–1].

You may also use mixed relative and absolute cell references. For example, $A1 and R[1]C1 have an absolute column reference and a relative row reference, or A$1 and R1C[1] have relative column references and absolute row references. The Formula Reference command can be used to cycle through the different reference types.

Naming Cells and Values

Using the Formula Define Name or the Formula Create Names commands, you can name numbers, strings, logical values, arrays of numbers, and formulas in Excel. Essentially, anything you can type into an edit box, you can define with a name, and wherever that name is placed, its definition will be used. The most common use of naming is for cell references. Once a cell reference has been named, you can use the name in place of the reference to make your formulas more readable.

A name must start with a letter and can contain any combination of letters, numbers and symbols. However, it cannot look like a cell reference. It also cannot contain spaces, so use a period or underscore as word separators.

Databases in Excel

A database in Excel is a rectangular region on the worksheet, each row of which is a record, and each column a field. The first row of the database must contain the field names. Once you have created the structure of the database, select the database, including the field names, and execute the Data Set Database command, or name it *Database* with the Formula Define Name command. You can now access this data with the database commands and functions.

To search a database, you must define a criteria range to contain the search criteria. The criteria range is also a rectangular region on the worksheet, at least two rows high. The first row contains the database field names to which you want to apply search criteria. The second and succeeding rows contain the search criteria. Excel assumes a logical AND between all criteria on the same row. That is, a record must satisfy all of the criteria on a row to be selected. A logical OR is assumed between criteria on different rows. That is, a record is selected if it satisfies the criteria on one row, or the criteria on a different row. Once you have setup a criteria range, select it and define it with the Data Set Criteria command, or name it *Criteria* with the Formula Define Name command.

The simplest criterion consists of some characters in a field in the criteria range. The search compares it to the same field in the database, ignoring capitalization. Excel will match every record that begins with those characters. You can also use wildcard characters to expand the comparison: * stands for any number of characters, and ? stands for any single character. To search for the * or ?, precede them with the tilde (~) character. To match text exactly, including capitalization, use the expression **="=Text"**. This will match records that contain only the characters *Text* in the specified field.

You can also use the comparison operators to search for ranges of records. For example, the criterion **>5000** will match every record that has a value greater than 5000 in that field. Since the = operator is also the formula flag, it must be enclosed in double quotes, as **="=text"**. The relational operators are

= equal to

> greater than

< less than

>= greater than or equal to

<= less than or equal to

<> not equal to

Criteria can be the results of string formulas. The value of the formula must look like one of the criteria described previously.

You can also compute a criterion from several fields. Create a new field name in the criteria range that is different from the field names in the database. In the second row of the criteria range, put a formula that evaluates to a logical value and uses the data from the first row of the database you want to examine. For example, if your database is in rows A10:G100, you could write a formula in your criteria range such as **=B11+D11<5**. This criterion would match any record in which the sum of the values in the second and fourth fields is less than 5. Note that the references are to the second row of the database, not the first row, which contains the field names.

One final range needs to be defined if you are planning to use the Data Extract command—an *extraction range,* which consists of a rectangular range at least one row high. The firsts row contains the names of the fields for which you want to extract data. If the extraction range consists of only one row containing the field names, the Data Extract command will extract all matching records in the database and insert the data below the field names in the extraction range. Be careful, because data below the extraction range can be overwritten. If the extraction range consists of more than one row, only that range will be filled with data. If there are more records than will fit in the range, Excel will tell you so.

Directory Paths

On the Macintosh, a directory path has, in order, the disk name, a colon-separated list of folder names, and then the file name. For example, **My Disk:Folder 1:Folder 2:My File** specifies that the document My File is in Folder 2, which is in Folder 1, on the disk named My Disk.

Navigating Dialog Boxes

Most of the commands in Excel open a dialog box to obtain the options and data required for the completion of the command. A dialog box is a rectangular box on the screen containing information, list boxes, edit boxes, buttons, radio buttons and check boxes.

A *list box* is a rectangular area that contains a list of available options for the command. For example, the File Open command displays a list of the files in the current directory.

An *edit box* contains text that can be edited with the keyboard. Edit boxes are used to get names and numbers for the commands. Often an edit box will be associated with a list box. When a list item is selected in the list box, it will appear in the edit box where it can be used as is or edited.

A *button* is a large, round-cornered rectangle with a title in the center. While all of the other boxes simply hold data, the buttons cause an action to take place. For example, the OK button generally executes a command, while the Cancel button discards the contents of the boxes and cancels the command.

Radio buttons are small round buttons that operate like the buttons on a radio. When one is selected, all the others in a group are deselected. They are used to select the mutually exclusive options that appear to their right. For example, you would select left-, right-, or center-justified text with one of three radio buttons.

Check boxes are small square boxes. They are checked with an X when selected. Check boxes are used to enable the non-exclusive options described in the text to their right.

There are also group boxes, which are rectangles drawn on the screen to group related options. In some cases, clicking on the group box title will reset the options to their default values.

Accessing Dialog Box Options Dialog boxes are primarily designed to be accessed with a mouse. However, they can be accessed from the keyboard. The Return key is equivalent to the button with the double border, which is usually the Open or OK button. Most buttons, radio buttons, and check boxes can be accessed by holding down the Command key and pressing the first letter in the button's name. If the dialog box contains a list box, you can select an element of the list by typing the first few characters of the items name, or by using the direction (Arrow) keys.

Hardware

Version 1.5 of Excel for the Macintosh requires at least 512K of memory and the 128K ROMs. That is, a 512KE, a Plus, an SE, an SE/30, a II or a IIx. While you can supposedly run Excel with one 400K disk drive, you won't like it. One 800K drive is about the minimum needed for reasonable operation. Two 800K drives or an 800K drive and a hard disk are needed for serious work.

Excel has problems accessing memory above 1 Mb. I would expect this to be corrected in the next update. Another apparent problem is that a custom startup screen may cause out-of-memory errors. This screen shows on the monitor when the Macintosh is booting up instead of the "Welcome to Macintosh" message. To remove it, look for a file named StartupScreen in the system folder of your startup disk. Change the name slightly, or move it to a different folder, and the startup screen will not be used.

Part 1:

Menu Commands and Macro Functions

All control and formatting of data in worksheets, macro sheets, and charts is performed with either menu commands or macro functions. This part will describe both of these. The first section lists the relatively few menu commands that have no equivalent macro functions. The second section contains an alphabetical list of the macro functions with a description of their operation and options.

Table 1.1 presents the menu commands in Macintosh Excel, cross referenced with their equivalent macro functions. To determine the operation of a particular menu command, find it in the list, and then look up its equivalent macro function. Also shown in the table is the mode of operation when a command is active. This mode depends on the type of document that is active. The codes used in the table are N (no documents open), W (worksheet or macro sheet active), and C (chart active).

An ellipsis (...) after a command name indicates that the command displays a dialog box.

MENU COMMAND	MODE	MACRO FUNCTION/ DESCRIPTION
Apple Menu	NWC	
About Excel...	NWC	none online help
File Menu	NWC	
New...	NWC	NEW() create new, blank document
Open...	NWC	OPEN() open document
Close All	WC	none close all open windows

Table 1.1: Menu Commands and equivalent macro functions

MENU COMMAND	MODE	MACRO FUNCTION/ DESCRIPTION
Links...	WC	OPEN.LINKS() open linked (referenced) documents CHANGE.LINKS()
Save	WC	SAVE() save document
Save As...	WC	SAVE.AS() save document with new name
Delete...	NWC	FILE.DELETE() delete disk file
Record Macro...	N	none record macro
Page Setup...	WC	PAGE.SETUP() set printing options
Print...	WC	PRINT() print active document
Printer Setup...	WC	PRINTER.SETUP() set printer options
Quit	NWC	QUIT() close all documents and quit Excel
Edit Menu	WC	
Undo	WC	UNDO() undo last action
Redo	WC	UNDO() reverse Undo

***Table 1.1:** Menu Commands and equivalent macro functions (continued)*

MENU COMMAND	MODE	MACRO FUNCTION/ DESCRIPTION
Cut	WC	CUT() mark selection for cutting
Copy	WC	COPY() mark selection for copying as data
Copy Picture	W	COPY.PICTURE() copy selection as picture (Shift-Copy)
Copy Chart	C	COPY.CHART() copy chart as picture
Paste	WC	PASTE() paste contents of copy or cut selection into current selection
Clear...	WC	CLEAR() clear contents of current selection
Paste Special...	WC	PASTE.SPECIAL() selective paste command
Delete...	W	EDIT.DELETE() delete selection and shift cells up or left to fill hole
Insert...	W	INSERT() insert some cells, shifting others down or right to make room

Table 1.1: Menu Commands and equivalent macro functions (continued)

MENU COMMAND	MODE	MACRO FUNCTION/ DESCRIPTION
Fill Right	W	FILL.RIGHT() copy cell contents on left of selection, right into rest of the selection
Fill Down	W	FILL.DOWN() copy cell contents at top of selection down into rest of selection
Formula Menu	W	
Paste Name...	W	none paste defined name at insertion point
Paste Function...	W	none paste function name at insertion point
Reference	W	none change reference type (absolute, relative)
Define Name...	W	DEFINE.NAME() define name as cell reference or value DELETE.NAME()
Create Names...	W	CREATE.NAMES() name cells according to text in cells to left or above them
Goto...	W	FORMULA.GOTO() make reference active cell, and scroll to it

Table 1.1: Menu Commands and equivalent macro functions (continued)

MENU COMMAND	MODE	MACRO FUNCTION/ DESCRIPTION
Find...	W	FORMULA.FIND() locate string in a cell
Select Last Cell	W	SELECT.LAST.CELL() select lower-right corner of used portion of worksheet
Show Active Cell	W	SHOW.ACTIVE.CELL() scroll to active cell
Format Menu (Worksheet version)	W	
Number...	W	FORMAT.NUMBER() set format and color for cell contents
Alignment...	W	ALIGNMENT() set alignment of values in cell
Style...	W	STYLE() set style (bold or italic) for cell contents
Border...	W	BORDER() put borders on cells
Cell Protection...	W	CELL.PROTECTION() mark cells to be locked or hidden
Column Width...	W	COLUMN.WIDTH() set width of columns

***Table 1.1:* Menu Commands and equivalent macro functions (continued)**

MENU COMMAND	MODE	MACRO FUNCTION/ DESCRIPTION
Format Menu (Chart version)	C	
Patterns...	C	none set line and area style, patterns, and color
Axis...	C	none set axis type and limits
Main Chart...	C	none set main chart options
Overlay Chart...	C	none set overlay chart options
Legend...	C	none set legend location
Text...	C	none set text font and size
Data Menu	W	
Find	W	DATA.FIND() find record that matches criteria
Extract...	W	EXTRACT() copy records that match criteria to selection
Delete	W	DATA.DELETE() delete record
Set Database	W	SET.DATABASE() define current selection as database

Table 1.1: Menu Commands and equivalent macro functions (continued)

MENU COMMAND	MODE	MACRO FUNCTION/ DESCRIPTION
Set Criteria	W	SET.CRITERIA() define current selection as criteria
Sort...	W	SORT() sort selection
Series...	W	DATA.SERIES() fill selection with sequence of numbers
Table...	W	TABLE() create table of values from formula (not on macro sheet)
Options Menu	W	
Set Print Area	W	SET.PRINT.AREA() define area to be printed
Set Print Titles	W	SET.PRINT.TITLES() define title area to be printed on every page
Set Page Break	W	SET.PAGE.BREAK() add page break
Remove Page Break	W	REMOVE.PAGE.BREAK() remove page break
Font...	W	none set text font and size
Display...	W	DISPLAY() set worksheet display options

Table 1.1: Menu Commands and equivalent macro functions (continued)

MENU COMMAND	MODE	MACRO FUNCTION/ DESCRIPTION
Freeze Panes	W	FREEZE.PANES() lock upper and left panes of split worksheet
Unfreeze Panes	W	FREEZE.PANES() unlock locked panes
Protect Document...	W	PROTECT.DOCUMENT() enable cell protection
Unprotect Document...	W	PROTECT.DOCUMENT() disable cell protection
Precision As Displayed	W	PRECISION() set numeric precision to precision as displayed
Full Precision	W	PRECISION() use full numeric precision
R1C1	W	A1.R1C1() set R1C1 style of cell referencing
A1	W	A1.R1C1() set A1 style of cell referencing
Calculate Now	W	CALCULATE.NOW() recalculate all open documents
Calculation...	W	CALCULATION() set automatic, manual, or iterated calculation

Table 1.1: Menu Commands and equivalent macro functions (continued)

MENU COMMAND	MODE	MACRO FUNCTION/ DESCRIPTION
Macro Menu	WC	
Run...	WC	RUN() run command macro
Record...	WC	none record macro
Set Recorder	W	none mark location for macro recording
Start Recorder	WC	none start recording macro
Stop Recorder	WC	none stop recording macro
Absolute Record	WC	none use absolute references when recording macro
Relative Record	WC	none use relative references when recording macro
Window Menu	WC	
Show Clipboard	WC	SHOW.CLIPBOARD() display contents of clipboard
New Window	W	NEW.WINDOW() create new window into open document
<Document List>	WC	ACTIVATE() activate selected document

Table 1.1: Menu Commands and equivalent macro functions (continued)

MENU COMMAND	MODE	MACRO FUNCTION/ DESCRIPTION
Gallery	C	
Area...	C	GALLERY.AREA() set area chart type
Bar...	C	GALLERY.BAR() set bar chart type
Column...	C	GALLERY.COLUMN() set column chart type
Line...	C	GALLERY.LINE() set line chart type
Pie...	C	GALLERY.PIE() set pie chart type
Scatter...	C	GALLERY.SCATTER() set scatter chart type
Combination...	C	COMBINATION() set combination chart type
Preferred	C	PREFERRED() format current chart with preferred format
Chart	C	
Main Chart Type...	C	MAIN.CHART.TYPE() set type of main chart
Overlay Chart Type...	C	OVERLAY.CHART.TYPE() set type of overlay chart
Set Preferred Format	C	none use active chart to define preferred format

Table 1.1: Menu Commands and equivalent macro functions (continued)

MENU COMMAND	MODE	MACRO FUNCTION/ DESCRIPTION
Axes...	C	none set which axes and grid lines are visible
Add Legend	C	LEGEND() add legend to a chart
Delete Legend	C	LEGEND() remove legend from chart
Attach Text...	C	none add attached text object to chart
Add Arrow	C	none add arrow to chart
Delete Arrow	C	none remove selected arrow
Select Chart	C	SELECT.CHART() select whole chart
Select Plot Area	C	none select plot area on chart
Calculate Now	C	CALCULATE.NOW() recalculate all open documents

Table 1.1: Menu Commands and equivalent macro functions (continued)

Menu Commands

The following section contains a description of the menus and commands that do not have equivalent macro functions.

Apple About Excel...

v: **ALL**

DIALOG BOX

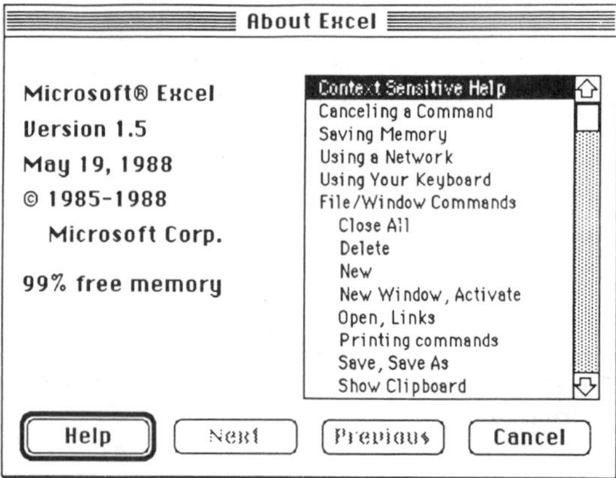

USAGE

The Apple menu is the first menu on the menu bar of all normal applications on the Apple Macintosh. It contains all of the desk accessories installed on the system. Desk accessories are small applications that run within larger applications, without having to quit the larger applications first. The only Excel command on the Apple menu is About Excel... .

The About Excel command opens the dialog box shown here, which shows the version, copyright, and available free memory. It also gives access to the online help facility. Topics discussed in the online help facility are listed in the list box on the right side of the dialog box. Select one and press the Help button (or double click the topic) to display the help topic.

Context-sensitive help is also available. Press **Command-?**, and the cursor will change into a question mark. Click on any object or menu command, and the help information for that object will be displayed.

The Next Button shows the next help topic. The Previous Button shows the previous help topic. The Cancel Button ends help.

Chart Add/Delete Arrow

v: **ALL**

USAGE

The Chart Add Arrow command places a new arrow on the active chart. The chart Delete Arrow command deletes the selected arrow.

Chart Attach Text...

v: ALL

DIALOG BOX

Attach Text
Attached to
Chart Title
Category Axis
Value Axis
Series or Data Point
Series Number:
Point Number:
OK
Cancel

USAGE

The Chart Attach Text command is used to add the chart title and axis labels. It is also used to attach text to a data point or series. The Chart Title radio button creates a text object at the top-center of the chart. The Category Axis radio button creates a text object along the bottom of the chart. The Value Axis radio button creates a text object on the left side of the chart. The Series or Data Point radio button attaches a text object to a data series or to a data point. For a text object attached to a series or data point, type the series number in the Series Number edit box and the point number in the Point Number edit box.

SEE ALSO

Format Text command, **Format Patterns** command

Chart Axes...

v: ALL

DIALOG BOX

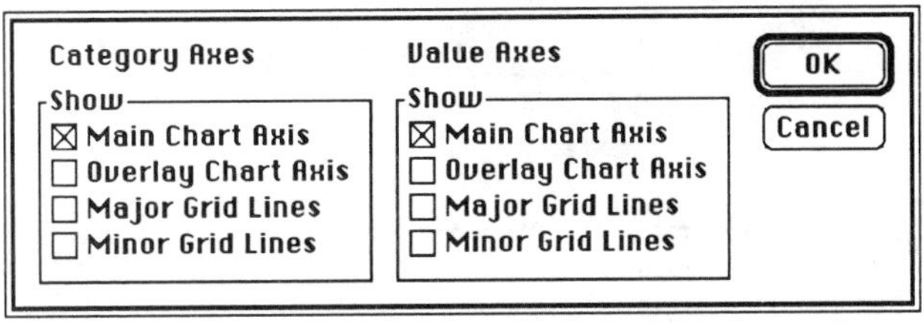

Category Axes

Show
- [x] Main Chart Axis
- [ ] Overlay Chart Axis
- [ ] Major Grid Lines
- [ ] Minor Grid Lines

Value Axes

Show
- [x] Main Chart Axis
- [ ] Overlay Chart Axis
- [ ] Major Grid Lines
- [ ] Minor Grid Lines

OK

Cancel

USAGE

The Chart Axes command controls the display of the axes and gridlines of the main chart, and of the overlay chart if it exists. If you display the overlay chart axes, be sure to execute the Format Overlay Chart Axis command and move the overlay chart axes away from the main chart axes. If a main chart axis and an overlay chart axis are at the same location, only the main chart axis will be displayed. In the dialog box, check the axes and the grid lines that you want displayed.

SEE ALSO

Format Main/Overlay Chart Axes command

Chart Set Preferred Format

v: **ALL**

USAGE

The Chart Set Preferred Format command changes the default chart format to that of the currently selected chart. All new charts are created with the default format, which is initially that of the first column chart under the Gallery menu.

SEE ALSO

Gallery Preferred command

File Close All

v: **ALL**

USAGE

When the File Close All command is executed, all windows are closed. To close a single window, use the close box on its upper-left corner.

SEE ALSO

CLOSE()

File Record Macro...

v: **1.5**

DIALOG BOX

See **Macro Record**

USAGE

This command is available in the File menu only when there are no open documents; otherwise, it is in the Macro menu named Record. It puts up a dialog box requesting a name and a keyboard shortcut command letter for a command macro, creates a new Macro sheet, and then begins recording the macro.

Format Axis...

v: ALL

DIALOG BOX

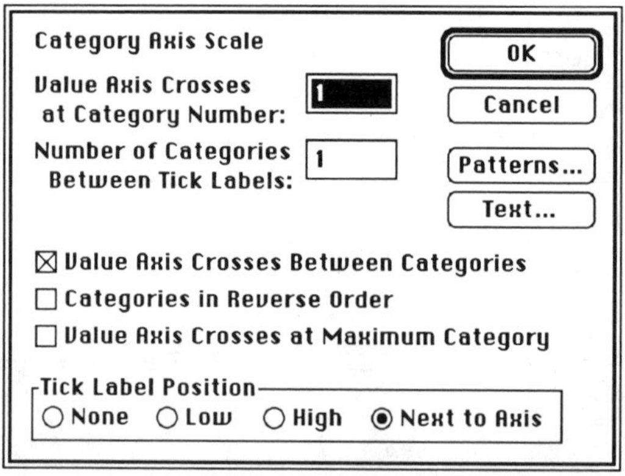

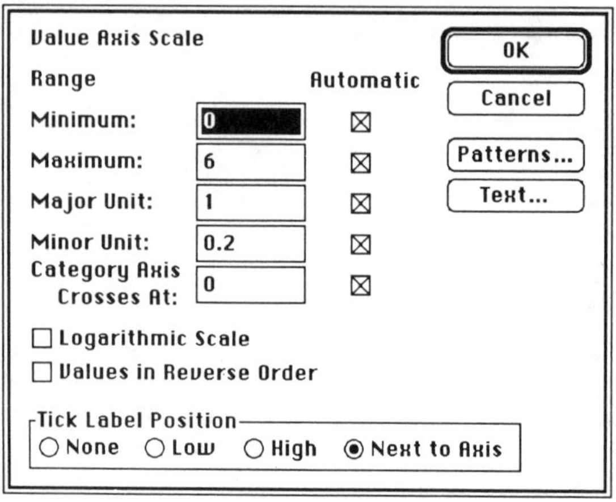

Category Axis Scale

Value Axis Crosses at Category Number: 1

Number of Categories Between Tick Labels: 1

OK

Cancel

Patterns...

Text...

☒ Value Axis Crosses Between Categories

☐ Categories in Reverse Order

☐ Value Axis Crosses at Maximum Category

Tick Label Position

○ None ○ Low ○ High ◉ Next to Axis

Value Axis Scale

Range | Automatic

Minimum: 0 ☒

Maximum: 6 ☒

Major Unit: 1 ☒

Minor Unit: 0.2 ☒

Category Axis Crosses At: 0 ☒

OK

Cancel

Patterns...

Text...

☐ Logarithmic Scale

☐ Values in Reverse Order

Tick Label Position

○ None ○ Low ○ High ◉ Next to Axis

USAGE

The Format Axis command is used to set the axis parameters for an axis of a chart. Set the limits, tick mark location, and axis crossing point with this command. Turn on the tick marks with the Format Patterns command.

There are two variations of this dialog box shown. The first is for the category axes on all charts but a scatter chart. The second is for the value axes on all charts, and the category axes on a scatter chart.

The Patterns button causes the Axis command to be executed and opens the Format Patterns dialog box. The Font button also causes the Axis command to be executed but opens the Format Font dialog box instead.

Insert the number of the category at which you want the value axis to cross in the Value Axis Crosses at Category Number edit box. The first category is number 1. Insert the number of categories to skip over when plotting labels on the tick marks on the axis in the Number of Categories Between Tick Labels edit box.

The Value Axis Crosses Between Categories check box puts the value axis between two categories instead of on top of one. The value axis will cross just before the category indicated in the Value Axis Crosses at Category Number edit box. The Categories in Reverse Order check box reverses the direction of the category axis. The Value Axis Crosses at Maximum Category check box makes the command ignore the Value Axis Crosses at Category Number edit box and puts the value axis on the right side of the chart (unless the Categories in Reverse Order check box is checked).

The Automatic check boxes lets Excel select the range values. Insert the lower limit for the axis in the Minimum edit box and the upper limit in the Maximum edit box. Insert the spacing between the major tick marks in the Major Unit edit box and the spacing between the minor tick marks in the Minor Unit edit box. Insert the value on the value axis where the category axis is to cross, or if a category axis is selected on a scatter chart, the value on the category axes where the value axis is to cross in the Category Axis Crosses At edit box.

The Logarithmic Scale check box makes the scale logarithmic instead of linear. The Values in Reverse Order check box reverses the direction of the value axis.

The None radio button removes the tick labels. The Low radio button puts the tick labels at the low end of the other axis. The High radio button puts the tick labels at the high end of the other axis. The Next to Axis radio button puts the tick labels next to the axis.

SEE ALSO

Format Patterns command, **Format Text** command

Format Legend...

v: **ALL**

DIALOG BOX

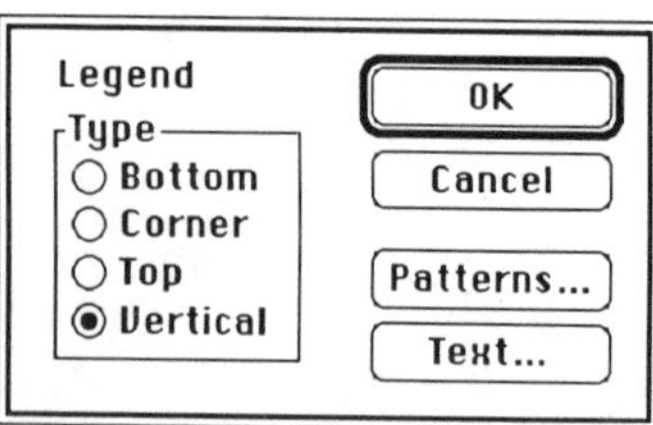

USAGE

The Format Legend command is used to set the location of a selected legend on a chart. The legend is initially created with the Chart Add Legend command. The Patterns button causes the Legend command to be executed and opens the Format Patterns dialog box. The Text button causes the Legend command to be executed and opens the Format Text dialog box.

The Bottom radio button places the legend along the bottom of the chart, the Corner radio button places it in the upper-right corner of the chart, the Top radio button places it along the top of the chart, and the Vertical radio button places it on the right side of the chart.

SEE ALSO

Chart Add Legend command, **Format Patterns** command, **Format Text** command

Format Main/Overlay Chart...

v: ALL

DIALOG BOX

Area Chart
☐ Stacked
☐ 100%
☐ Drop Lines
OK
Cancel
First Series in Overlay Chart: 1
☒ Automatic Series Distribution

Line Chart
☐ Stacked
☐ 100%
☐ Vary by Categories
☐ Drop Lines
☐ Hi-Lo Lines
OK
Cancel
First Series in Overlay Chart: 1
☒ Automatic Series Distribution

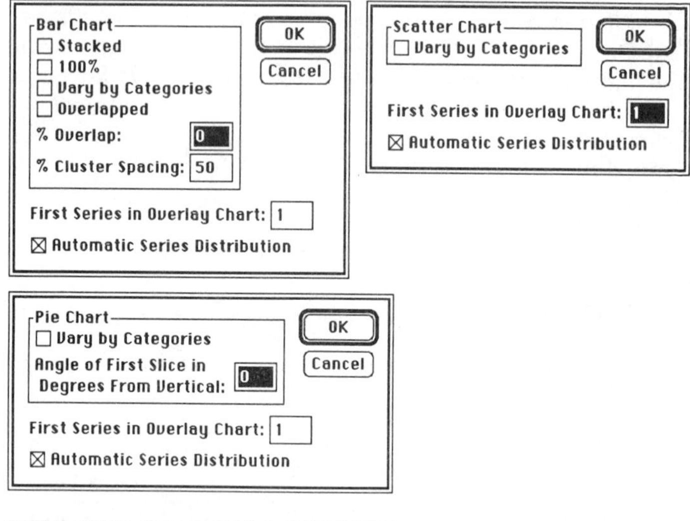

USAGE

Excel allows you to split the plotting of your data series between two different chart types. The first, or default, is the main chart. The second is the overlay chart. The Format Main Chart command is used to set the style parameters for the main chart. Set the type of the main chart with the Chart Main Chart Type command. The Format Overlay Chart command does the same for the overlay chart. Set the overlay chart type with the Chart Overlay Chart Type command.

There are six different dialog boxes for the Format Main Chart command, depending on the type of the active chart. The Format Overlay chart command has an additional six, which are nearly identical to the main chart dialog boxes. Only five are shown here, as the options for the bar and column charts are identical. The dialog boxes shown are for the overlay charts. The main chart dialog boxes lack the First Series in Overlay Chart edit box, and the Automatic Series Distribution check box.

The Stacked check box causes the values in each series to be added to the values of those already plotted on the chart. When a chart contains a single data series, the Vary by Categories check box causes each data point to have a different marker. The Drop Lines check box causes drop lines to be inserted from the highest value in each series to the category axis. The 100% check box causes the values at each category to be plotted as a percent of the sum of all of the values at that category. The Overlapped check box causes bars or columns to be overlapped. The Hi-Lo lines check box causes a line to extend from the highest value to the lowest value at each category.

In the % Overlap edit box insert the percent overlap of bars or columns at a category if the Overlapped check box is checked. If the box is not checked, insert the percent separation of bars or columns. In the % Cluster Spacing edit box, insert the spacing between one category and another. In the Angle of First Pie Slice edit box insert the angle, clockwise in degrees, of the upper edge of the first pie slice in a pie chart.

In the First Series in Overlay Chart edit box insert the number of the first series to appear in the overlay chart. All series numbers equal to or greater than this number will be in the overlay chart. The Automatic Series distribution check box causes the command to ignore the First Series in Overlay Chart edit box, and to evenly split the series between the main and overlay charts. If the number of data series is odd, the main chart will have one more series than the overlay chart.

SEE ALSO

MAIN.CHART.TYPE(), OVERLAY.CHART.TYPE()

Format Patterns...

v: ALL

DIALOG BOX

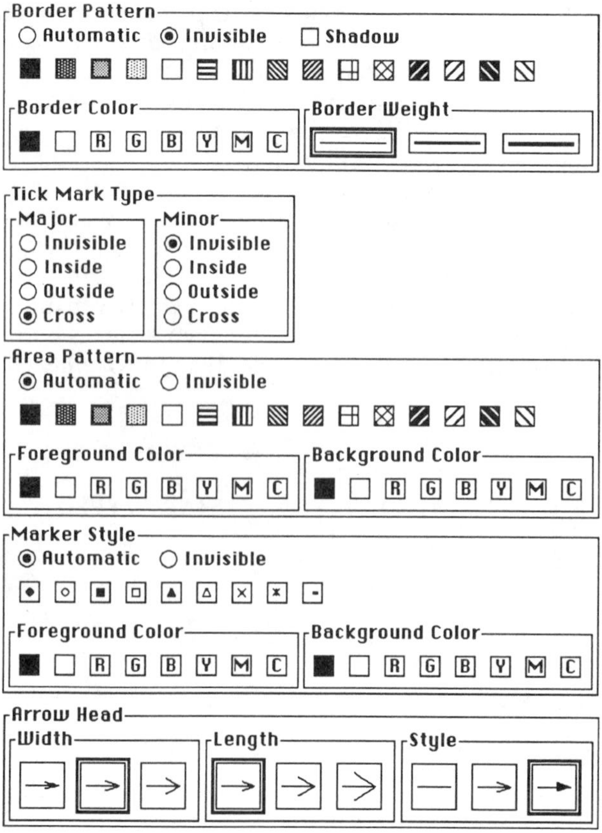

Border Pattern
○ Automatic ◉ Invisible ☐ Shadow

Border Color
■ ☐ R G B Y M C

Border Weight

Tick Mark Type
Major
○ Invisible
○ Inside
○ Outside
◉ Cross

Minor
◉ Invisible
○ Inside
○ Outside
○ Cross

Area Pattern
◉ Automatic ○ Invisible

Foreground Color
■ ☐ R G B Y M C

Background Color
■ ☐ R G B Y M C

Marker Style
◉ Automatic ○ Invisible

Foreground Color
■ ☐ R G B Y M C

Background Color
■ ☐ R G B Y M C

Arrow Head
Width
Length
Style

USAGE

The Format Patterns command is used to set the patterns and colors of objects on charts. Select an object on a chart and execute the Patterns command, and a dialog box will appear containing the pattern boxes shown above that are relevant to the selected object. Double clicking on a chart object will also call up the Format Patterns dialog box.

The Format Patterns dialog box has five different variations, depending on what has been selected on a chart. If the selection is the whole chart, the plot area, the legend, any text label, an area in an area or pie chart, or a bar on a bar or column chart, the dialog box will consist of a Border Pattern and an Area Pattern box. If the selection is an axis, the dialog box will consist of a Border Pattern and a Tick Mark box. If the selection is a gridline, hilo line, or drop line, the dialog box will consist of only a Border Pattern box. If the selection consists of a data line or marker, the dialog box will consist of a Border Pattern and a Marker Style box. Finally, if the selection consists of an arrow, the dialog box will consist of a Border Pattern and an Arrow Head box.

Depending on the formatting options available to the selected chart object, some of the following buttons will also be in the dialog box. The Text button causes the Patterns command to be executed and opens the Format Text dialog box. The Axis button causes the Patterns command to be executed and opens the Format Axis dialog box. The Legend button causes the Patterns command to be executed and opens the Format Legend dialog box.

The Apply to All check box causes the Patterns command to be applied to all similar objects, such as, all the data points in a series.

The Border Pattern box, with slight variations, is alternately known as an Axis Pattern box, Line Pattern box, Arrow Pattern box, Line box, or Arrow Shaft box. It contains formatting commands for lines. The Automatic radio button lets Excel select the line color and style. The Invisible radio button makes the lines invisible. The Shadow check box shadows lines that are outlines of areas such as the whole chart or the outline of the legend. Select the pattern for the line or border from the Border

Pattern list. Select the color for the lines from the Border Color list. The colors are black, white, red, green, blue, yellow, magenta, and cyan. Select the desired thickness of the lines from the Border Weight list.

The Tick Mark Type box sets the type of tick marks on an axis. Selections in the Major box apply to the major tick marks. Only the major tick marks have labels. Selections in the Minor box apply to the minor tick marks. The Invisible radio button hides the tick marks. The Inside radio button puts the tick marks inside of the axis. The Outside radio button puts the tick marks outside of the axis. The Cross radio button makes the tick marks cross the axis.

The Area Pattern box is also known as the Background Pattern box. It contains the patterns for area and bars. Select the fill pattern for the area from the Area Pattern list. Select the color for the foreground of the pattern from the Foreground Color list. Select the color for the background of the pattern from the Background Color list.

The Marker Style box sets the shape and color of data markers. The Automatic radio button lets Excel use different markers for different series. The Invisible radio button makes the markers invisible. Be careful—if you have invisible lines and invisible markers, you will not be able to select a data series. Select the marker to use for the selected data series from the Marker Style list. Select the color for the foreground of the markers from the Foreground Color list. Select the color for the background of the markers from the Background Color list.

The Arrow Head box is used to set the size and shape of an arrowhead. Select the width of the arrowhead to use from the width list, the length of the arrowhead from the Length list, and the style of the arrowhead from the Style list.

SEE ALSO

Format Axis command, **Format Text** command, **Format Legend** command

Format Text...

v: **ALL**

DIALOG BOX

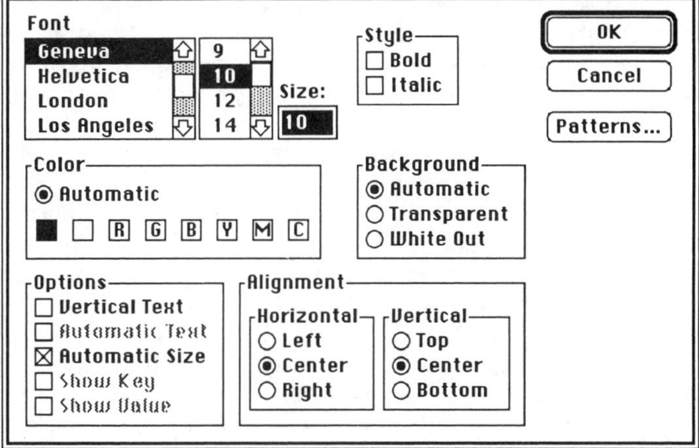

USAGE

The Format Text command controls the font, style and alignment of the selected text object on a chart. The dialog box shown is for any chart text object but an axis or a legend, which do not have the Alignment radio buttons or Options check boxes. The buttons on the right side also change, depending on what other formatting options are available for the selected text object.

The Patterns button causes the Text command to be executed, and opens the Format Patterns dialog box. The Legend button causes the Text command to be executed and opens the Format Legend dialog box. The Axis button causes the Text command to be executed and opens the Format Axis dialog box.

The Font list box shows the list of fonts available. Select the font you want from this list. The Size list box shows the available sizes of the selected font. In the Size edit box insert the size of the font to use, or select it from the Size list.

The Bold check box makes the font bold. The Italic check box makes the font italic. The Automatic radio button lets Excel pick the background for you. The Transparent radio button makes the background of the text transparent so that you can see what is behind it. The White Out radio button blanks out anything behind the text. Select the text color from the Color list, or select automatic color selection. The colors are black, white, red, green, blue, yellow, magenta, and cyan. While the colors will not show on a black-and-white Macintosh, they will appear on the output if you have a color printer.

The Vertical Text check box causes the text to be stacked vertically. This is not rotated text, but normally oriented characters stacked one above the other. The Automatic Text check box returns attached text objects that were edited to the original text. The Automatic Size check box makes the border just fit the text it contains. This only applies to unattached text, since you cannot change the border of attached text. The Show Key check box puts a copy of the data marker to the left of the text of an attached text object. The Show Value check box, combined with the Automatic Text check box, replaces the text attached to a data point with the value of that point.

The Alignment radio buttons (Left, Center, Right, Top, Center, Bottom) set the vertical and horizontal alignment of text within its border rectangle.

Formula Paste Function...

v: ALL

DIALOG BOX

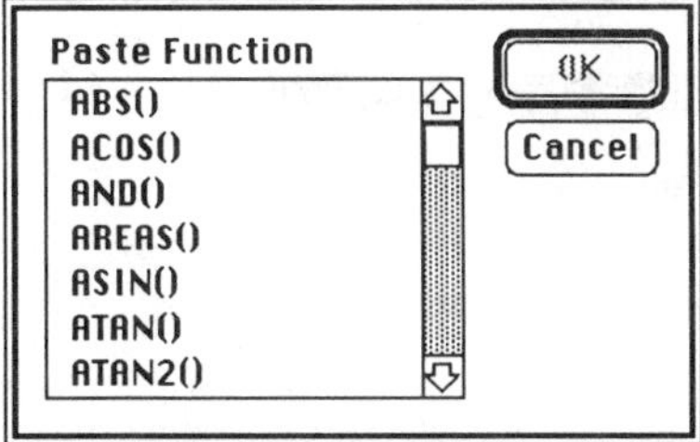

USAGE

The Formula Paste Function command inserts the selected function at the insertion point in the formula bar and leaves the insertion point between the parentheses. This function is most useful for pasting references to user-defined function macros. Such functions can often be difficult to insert, because they must include the external reference to the macro sheet as well as the function name.

The Paste Function list box shows a list of all of the functions available on the active document, including defined function macros on open macro sheets.

Formula Paste Name...

v: **ALL**

DIALOG BOX

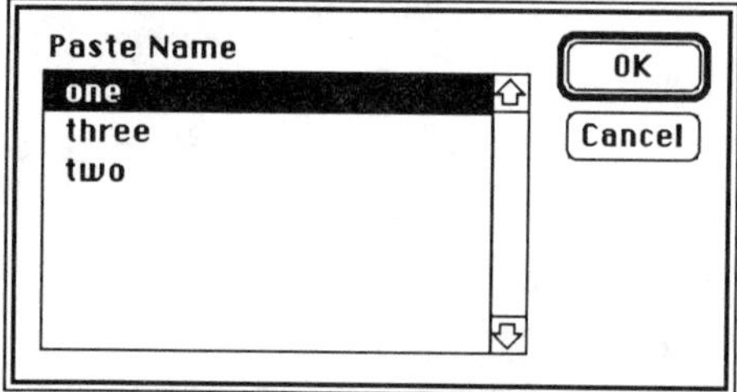

USAGE

The Formula Paste Name command allows you to paste a defined name at the insertion point in the formula bar. This command is primarily used to insure that you use a name defined on the active document, and that you spell it correctly. Select the name you want in the Paste Name list box, which contains all of the defined names on the active worksheet.

SEE ALSO

CREATE.NAMES(), DEFINE.NAME(), Formula Paste Function command

Formula Reference

v: ALL

USAGE

The Formula Reference command changes the type of the selected reference in the formula bar. You can select the reference by dragging across it or by having the edit cursor in it. If several references are selected, all of them will be changed at the same time. The reference types will change among relative (A1), absolute (A1), relative column-absolute row (A$1), relative row-absolute column ($A1), and back to relative (A1).

Macro Absolute/Relative Record

v: ALL

USAGE

The Macro Absolute Record command sets the macro recorder to use absolute cell references when recording. Normally the macro recorder uses relative references when recording macro functions. The Macro Relative Record command sets the macro recorder to use relative cell references when recording a macro.

SEE ALSO

Macro Record command, **Macro Set Recorder** command, **Macro Start Recorder** command, **Macro Stop Recorder** command

Macro Record...

v: **ALL**

DIALOG BOX

Macro Recorder

Name: Record1

Option-⌘ Key: a

OK

Cancel

USAGE

The Macro Record command is used for automatically recording macros. When executed, it puts up a dialog box requesting a name and shortcut command letter for a command macro, creates a new macro sheet, and then begins recording the macro. Perform the actions you want to record, and then stop the recording with the Macro Stop Recorder command.

SEE ALSO

Macro Set Recorder command, **Macro Start Recorder** command, **Macro Stop Recorder** command, **Macro Relative Record** command

Macro Set Recorder

v: ALL

USAGE

The Macro Set Recorder command marks the starting point for recording the next macro. Select the cell or range on a macro sheet where you want to begin recording, and execute the command. Recording will not start until you execute the Macro Start Recorder command.

If the selection is a single cell, all the cells below it become the recorder range. If the selection is a range of cells, only that range is the recorder range. If the recorder range contains data, recording will begin in the first cell below the last cell containing data, unless the last cell contains =RETURN(), in which case the last cell will be overwritten.

SEE ALSO

Macro Absolute Record command, **Macro Start Recorder** command, **Macro Stop Recorder** command

Macro Start Recorder

v: ALL

USAGE

The Macro Start Recorder command starts the macro recorder. Macro commands will start being recorded at the place specified with the Macro Set Recorder command.

SEE ALSO

Macro Absolute/Relative Record command, **Macro Record** command, **Macro Set Recorder** command, **Macro Stop Recorder** command

Macro Stop Recorder

v: ALL

USAGE

The Macro Stop Recorder command records an =RETURN() statement, and then stops recording of macro functions started with the Macro Start recorder command.

SEE ALSO

Macro Absolute/Relative Record command, **Macro Record** command, **Macro Set Recorder** command, **Macro Start Recorder** command

Options Font...

v: ALL

DIALOG BOX

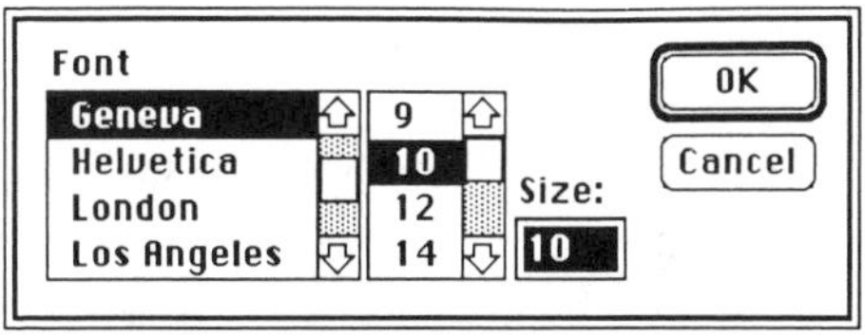

USAGE

The Options Font command controls the font used on the worksheet. The Font list box shows the list of available fonts. Select the font you want to use to display the contents of cells, and for row and column headings. The Size list box shows the available sizes of the selected font. Type the size of the font that you want into the Size text edit box, or select it in the Size list box. If you type a font size that is not in the Size list box, Excel will convert one of the existing sizes. Converted font sizes are often ragged.

SEE ALSO

Format Text command, **STYLE()**

Macro Functions

Your first impression of a macro sheet is that it looks the same as a worksheet. Functionally, though, it is quite different. On a worksheet, calculation proceeds in a dependent order. Cells that are referenced by other cells are calculated first, then the cells that depend on them. Calculations in a macro sheet proceed statement by statement down a column. References on a macro sheet evaluate to the current value of the referenced cell and do not force the calculation of cells on which the referenced cells depend.

Macros on the macro sheet are computer programs, completely analogous to those written in BASIC, C, or some other modern programming language. Most of the capabilities of those modern languages are available in the Excel macro language. However, the macro language also has access to all of the commands and functions of the worksheets. A macro can be written to use the BASIC-like sequential approach to calculate some number, or it can use a semi-parallel calculation by creating a worksheet to calculate it.

All of the worksheet functions described in Part 2, as well as all of the macro functions in this part, are allowed on a macro sheet. Although worksheet functions can be used on a macro sheet, macro functions cannot be used on a worksheet.

This section contains a complete alphabetical list of the macro functions and commands available in Excel.

Many of the macro functions that are equivalent to commands have a *NAME?()* form, which brings up the command dialog box instead of taking arguments. The options are then selected in the dialog box. There are no arguments allowed in these forms.

Table 1.2 contains a list of all of the macro commands and functions.

NAME	DESCRIPTION
File Input/Output	
CHANGE.LINK()	change links to other worksheets
CLOSE()	close active window
DIRECTORY()	set and return path to current directory
DOCUMENTS()	list open documents
FILE.DELETE()	delete disk file
FILES()	list files in current directory
GET.DOCUMENT()	return information about document
LINKS()	list documents referenced by this document
OPEN()	open document
OPEN.LINKS()	open list of documents
SAVE()	save document
SAVE.AS()	save document with new name
QUIT()	close all documents and quit Excel
Printing	
PAGE.SETUP()	set printing options
PRINT()	print active document
PRINTER.SETUP()	set printer options
REMOVE.PAGE.BREAK()	remove page break
SET.PAGE.BREAK()	add page break
SET.PRINT.AREA()	define area to be printed
SET.PRINT.TITLES()	define title area to be printed on every page

Table 1.2: Macro functions by type

NAME	DESCRIPTION
Worksheet Editing	
CANCEL.COPY()	cancel selection marquee set with COPY()
CLEAR()	clear contents of cells in selection
COPY()	mark selection for copying as data
COPY.PICTURE()	copy selection as picture
CUT()	mark selection for cutting
DATA.SERIES()	fill selection with sequence of numbers
EDIT.DELETE()	delete selection and shift cells up or left to fill in hole
FILL.DOWN()	copy cell contents at top of selection down into rest of selection
FILL.RIGHT()	copy cell contents on left of selection right into rest of selection
FORMULA()	insert value or formula into cell
FORMULA.ARRAY()	insert array formula into array of cells.
FORMULA.FILL()	insert value or formula into array of cells
FORMULA.GOTO()	make reference active cell and scroll worksheet until visible
INSERT()	insert some cells, shifting others down or right to make room

Table 1.2: Macro functions by type (continued)

NAME	DESCRIPTION
PASTE()	paste contents of COPY() or CUT() selection into current selection
PASTE.SPECIAL()	selective paste command
SELECT()	set selection and active cell
SELECT.LAST.CELL()	select lower-right corner of used part of worksheet
SORT()	sort selection
TABLE()	create table of values from formula
Worksheet Formatting	
ALIGNMENT()	set alignment of values in cell
BORDER()	put borders on cells
COLUMN.WIDTH()	set width of columns
DELETE.FORMAT()	delete custom numeric format
FONT()	select font for worksheet
FORMAT.NUMBER()	set format and color for cell contents
FREEZE.PANES()	lock upper and left panes of split worksheet
STYLE()	set style (bold or italic) for cell contents
UNLOCKED.NEXT()	scroll to next unlocked cell
UNLOCKED.PREV()	scroll back to previous unlocked cell
Reference Manipulation	
ABSREF()	change relative to absolute reference

Table 1.2: Macro functions by type (continued)

NAME	DESCRIPTION
ACTIVE.CELL()	return reference of active cell
CREATE.NAMES()	name cells according to text in cells to left or above
DEFINE.NAME()	define name as cell reference or value
DELETE.NAME()	delete defined name
DEREF()	return contents of reference
FORMULA.FIND()	locate cell containing string
FORMULA.FIND.NEXT()	find next cell containing string
FORMULA.FIND.PREV()	back up to previous cell containing string
GET.CELL()	return information about cell
GET.DEF()	return name of definition
GET.DOCUMENT()	return information about document
GET.FORMULA()	return contents of cell
GET.NAME()	return definition of name
GET.WINDOW()	return information about window
LINKS()	list documents linked to this document
OFFSET()	return offset reference
REFTEXT()	convert reference to string
RELREF()	convert absolute to relative reference
SELECT()	set selection and active cell
SELECTION()	return current selection
SET.NAME()	define name on macro sheet

Table 1.2: Macro functions by type (continued)

NAME	DESCRIPTION
SET.VALUE()	set value of cell on macro sheet
TEXTREF()	convert string to reference
Chart Formatting	
COMBINATION()	set combination chart type
COPY()	copy chart as data
COPY.CHART()	copy chart as picture
FORMULA()	attach data and text items
GALLERY.AREA()	set area chart type
GALLERY.BAR()	set bar chart type
GALLERY.COLUMN()	set column chart type
GALLERY.LINE()	set line chart type
GALLERY.PIE()	set pie chart type
GALLERY.SCATTER()	set scatter chart type
GET.DOCUMENT()	return information about document
LEGEND()	add or delete legend
MAIN.CHART.TYPE()	set type of main chart
OVERLAY.CHART.TYPE()	set type of overlay chart
PREFERRED()	make current chart's format preferred format
SELECT.CHART()	select whole chart
Custom Menus	
ADD.BAR()	create new menu bar
ADD.COMMAND()	add command to menu
ADD.MENU()	add menu to menu bar

Table 1.2: Macro functions by type (continued)

NAME	DESCRIPTION
CHECK.COMMAND()	add or remove check mark on command
DELETE.BAR()	delete custom menu bar
DELETE.COMMAND()	delete custom command from menu
DELETE.MENU()	delete custom menu from menu bar
ENABLE.COMMAND()	enable (black) or disable (gray) command on menu
GET.BAR()	return number of current menu bar
RENAME.COMMAND()	change name of command on menu
SHOW.BAR()	make specified menu bar current
Custom Dialog Boxes and Messages	
ALERT()	display alert box
DIALOG.BOX()	display custom dialog box
INPUT()	display input dialog box
MESSAGE()	display message
Macro Control	
ARGUMENT()	define arguments for function macro
BREAK()	exit FOR()/NEXT() or WHILE()/NEXT() loop
CALLER()	get reference of calling routine
DEFINE.NAME()	define and name command and function macros

Table 1.2: Macro functions by type (continued)

NAME	DESCRIPTION
ERROR()	enable or disable macro error checking
FOR()	start of counted loop
GOTO()	nonreturning branch in macro
HALT()	halt macro and return to Ready mode
NEXT()	bottom of FOR() or WHILE() loop
ref() (see SUBROUTINES)	execute function macro
RESULT()	set type of value returned by function macro
RETURN()	end function macro and return to caller
RUN()	run command macro
STEP()	begin single-step execution of macro
WHILE()	start of logically terminated loop
Database Manipulation	
DATA.DELETE()	delete record
DATA.FIND()	find any record that matches criteria
DATA.FIND.NEXT()	find next record that matches criteria
DATA.FIND.PREV()	back up to previous record that matched criteria
EXTRACT()	copy records that match criteria to selection
SET.CRITERIA()	define current selection as criteria

Table 1.2: Macro functions by type (continued)

NAME	DESCRIPTION
SET.DATABASE()	define current selection as database
Window Information and Control	
ACTIVATE()	make specific window active
ACTIVATE.NEXT()	activate next window down on desktop
ACTIVATE.PREV()	activate bottom window on desktop
DOCUMENTS()	list open documents
FULL()	expand window to full size
GET.WINDOW()	return information about window
HLINE()	scroll horizontally by columns
HPAGE()	scroll horizontally by pages
HSCROLL()	scroll horizontally to specific column
MOVE()	move a window
NEW()	create new blank document
NEW.WINDOW()	create new window into open document
SHOW.ACTIVE.CELL()	scroll to active cell
SHOW.CLIPBOARD()	display contents of clipboard
SIZE()	change size of window
SPLIT()	split window into panes
VLINE()	scroll vertically by rows
VPAGE()	scroll vertically by pages

Table 1.2: Macro functions by type (continued)

NAME	DESCRIPTION
VSCROLL()	scroll vertically to specific row
WINDOWS()	list open windows
Environment	
A1.R1C1()	set A1 or R1C1 style of cell referencing
CALCULATE.NOW()	recalculate all open documents
CALCULATION()	set automatic, manual, or iterated calculation
CELL.PROTECTION()	mark cells to be locked or hidden
DISPLAY()	set worksheet display options
ECHO()	enable or disable screen updating
GET.WORKSPACE()	return information about environment
PRECISION()	set full precision, or precision as displayed
PROTECT.DOCUMENT()	enable or disable cell protection
Other	
BEEP()	sound system beep
QUIT()	close all windows and quit Excel
UNDO()	reverse last action
WAIT()	pause macro until specific time

Note: A few macro functions appear in more than one category.

Table 1.2: Macro functions by type (continued)

A1.R1C1()

v: **ALL**

SYNTAX

A1.R1C1(<*logical*>**)**

EQUIVALENT COMMAND

Options A1 and **Options R1C1**

USAGE

The A1.R1C1() function sets the method of referencing used on the worksheets and macro sheets. Its argument is a logical value. If it is TRUE, the A1 referencing method is used. If it is FALSE, the R1C1 method is used. In the A1 method, columns are marked with letters and rows are marked with numbers. Hence, A1 stands for the cell in column A and row 1. In the R1C1 form, R stands for row and C stands for column, so R1C1 stands for the cell at row 1 and column 1.

Excel normally uses the A1 style. For more information on cell referencing, see the Introduction.

ABSREF()

v: ALL

SYNTAX

ABSREF(<*relative_reference_string*>,<*reference*>**)**

EQUIVALENT COMMAND

None

USAGE

The ABSREF() macro function gives the reference of a cell that is offset from <*reference*> according to the relative cell reference in the string <*relative_reference_string*>. The <*relative_reference_string*> string must be a relative reference in the R1C1 style of cell referencing. For more information on cell references, see the Introduction.

The RELREF() macro function can be used to create relative reference strings in the R1C1 from A1- or R1C1-style references.

SEE ALSO

RELREF()

ACTIVATE[.*xxxx*]()

v: **ALL**

SYNTAX

ACTIVATE([<*window*>][,<*pane_number*>]**)**
ACTIVATE.NEXT()
ACTIVATE.PREV()

EQUIVALENT COMMAND

None, but see below

USAGE

The ACTIVATE() macro function is equivalent to clicking in a window. If <*window*> is omitted, the current window is assumed. If the window has been split into more than one pane using the split bar, <*pane_number*> determines which pane is active. The allowed values are 1 (top-left), 2 (top-right), 3 (bottom-left), and 4 (bottom-right). If <*pane_number*> is omitted, the pane is not changed from the last time the window was active. This function is primarily used with the VSCROLL(), HSCROLL(), and GOTO() macro functions, to select the pane on which these functions act.

The windows in Excel sit in a pile on the desktop. The ACTIVATE.NEXT() macro function puts the current window on the bottom of the pile, and then activates the next window. The ACTIVATE.PREV() macro function does just the opposite, moving the window on the bottom of the pile to the top and activating it.

Note that the argument <*pane_number*> is in Version 1.5 or later.

Use the WINDOWS() macro function to get a list of window names as an array of strings, and use the INDEX() function to select a particular window name from that array.

SEE ALSO

GOTO(), HSCROLL(), VSCROLL(), WINDOWS()

ACTIVE.CELL()

v: **ALL**

SYNTAX

ACTIVE.CELL()

EQUIVALENT COMMAND

None

USAGE

The ACTIVE.CELL() macro function returns the reference of the active cell, as an external reference. By contrast, the SELECTION() macro function returns the reference of the current selection. An external reference includes the name of the document as well as the cell reference.

Note that while this function returns a reference, if you put it in a cell and execute it, what you will have in the cell is the contents of the reference. To see the reference instead of its contents, convert it to text with the REFTEXT() macro function.

SEE ALSO

REFTEXT(), SELECTION()

ADD.BAR()

v: 1.5

SYNTAX

ADD.BAR()

EQUIVALENT COMMAND

None

USAGE

The ADD.BAR() macro function creates a new blank menu bar and returns a *bar_number* reference to it. You must use ADD.MENU() to add menus to it, ADD.COMMAND() to add commands to the menus, and SHOW.BAR() to display it.

In Excel, you have the capability of creating custom menu bars and menus. Use them to give yourself immediate access to often-used macros. If Excel lacks a command that you believe to be important, create the command as a macro and add it to a menu in one of Excel's built-in menu bars. The menus that you create will have all of the capabilities of standard Excel menus. Menu commands can be disabled or checked and can have Command Key equivalents. See the ADD.MENU() macro function for more information.

Macintosh Excel has three built-in menu bars: the *worksheet and macro sheet* bar, the *chart* bar, and the *nil* bar.

The worksheet and macro sheet bar is the one that you see when a worksheet or macro sheet is active. It consists of the menus

File Edit Formula Format Data Options Macro Window

The chart bar is the one you see when a chart is active. It consists of the menus

File Edit Gallery Chart Format Macro Window

The nil bar is the one you see when there is no open document or active desk accessory. It consists of the menus

File Edit Window

These three menu bars have *bar_numbers* 1, 2, and 3, respectively. Any new menu bars that you create will be in addition to these. Bar numbers 4 through 6 are reserved for future versions of Excel, so the first custom menu bar will be number 7. You do not need to create a new menu bar with the ADD.BAR() macro function to add a new menu to a spreadsheet. You may add additional menus to any of the three built-in menu bars.

SEE ALSO

ADD.COMMAND(), ADD.MENU(), CHECK.COMMAND(), DELETE.BAR(), DELETE.COMMAND(), DELETE.MENU(), ENABLE.COMMAND(), GET.BAR(), RENAME.COMMAND(), SHOW.BAR()

ADD.COMMAND()

v: **1.5**

SYNTAX

ADD.COMMAND(*<bar_number>***,***<menu_position>***,** *<command_reference>***)**

EQUIVALENT COMMAND

None

USAGE

The ADD.COMMAND() macro function is used to add a new command to an existing menu. It returns the line number where the first command in *<command_reference>* is inserted. Successive commands in *<command_reference>* are added to the following lines in the menu.

The allowed values for *<bar_number>* are 1 through 21. Values 1 through 3 are for Excel's built-in menu bars, values 4 through 6 are reserved for future versions of Excel, and values 7 through 21 are for custom menu bars. See the **ADD.-BAR()** macro function for more information about built-in and custom menu bars.

<menu_ position> is the menu on the menu bar to add the command to, entered as a string containing the menu name or the number of its position. The Apple menu is not counted.

<command_reference> is a reference to a command definition table. A command definition table is identical to a menu definition table without the first line that contains the menu name (see the ADD.MENU() macro function). The reference can be external.

SEE ALSO

ADD.BAR(), ADD.MENU(), CHECK.COMMAND(), DELETE.BAR(), DELETE.COMMAND(), DELETE.MENU(), ENABLE.COMMAND(), GET.BAR(), RENAME.COMMAND(), SHOW.BAR()

ADD.MENU()

v: **1.5**

SYNTAX

ADD.MENU(*<bar_number>*,*<menu_reference>*)

EQUIVALENT COMMAND

None

USAGE

The ADD.MENU() macro function adds a menu to an existing menu bar. The function returns the position of the new menu on the menu bar.

<bar_number> is the menu bar to add the menu to, entered as an integer. The allowed values are 1 through 21. Values 1 through 3 are for Excel's built-in menu bars. Values 4 through 6 are reserved for future versions. Values 7 through 21 are for custom menu bars. See the **ADD.BAR()** macro function for more information about menu bars.

<menu_reference> is a reference to a menu definition table. The reference can be external.

A menu is defined with a menu definition table, such as that shown here in cells A6 through C11.

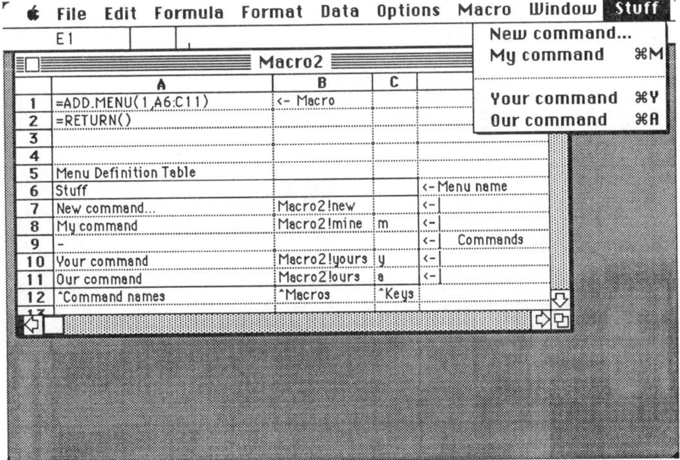

The first row of the menu definition table contains the name of the menu. It should be a short, single word to conserve space on the menu bar. Next are one or more command definitions. The command definition consists of the command name, the command macro, and an optional shortcut key, each in a separate column.

The command name can be more than one word, but should not be too long. It is common practice to put ellipses (...) after command names that will display a dialog box. A hyphen instead of a command name will place a horizontal bar across the menu. The second column contains references to the command macros that you want executed when the commands are selected. These references must be external, even if the macros are on the same macro sheet as the menu definition table. The third column contains an optional short cut key. Pressing this key while holding down the Command key is the same as selecting the command from the menu. Make sure that a short-cut key is used only once on a menu bar. If you use a short-cut key that is the same as one of Excel's built-in keys, your command will be executed instead of Excel's.

SEE ALSO

ADD.BAR(), ADD.COMMAND(), CHECK.COMMAND(), DELETE.BAR(), DELETE.COMMAND(), DELETE.MENU(), ENABLE.COMMAND(), GET.BAR(), RENAME.COMMAND(), SHOW.BAR()

ALERT()

***v:* ALL**

DIALOG BOX

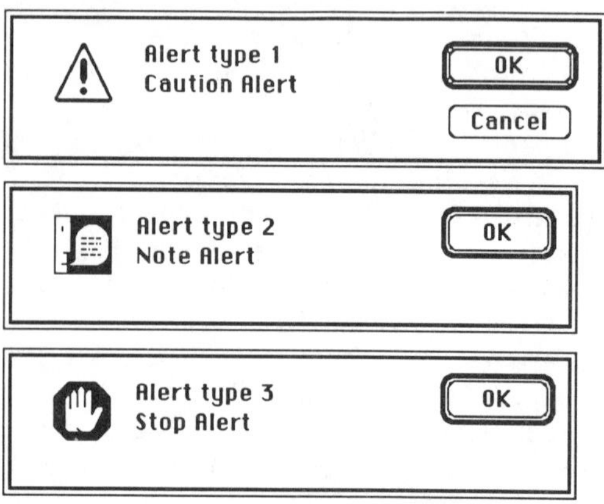

SYNTAX

ALERT(*<message_string>*,*<alert_type>*)

EQUIVALENT COMMAND

None

USAGE

The ALERT() macro function displays *<message_string>* in one of three alert boxes. Enter *<message_string>* as a string. You can insert a string any length, but only about 50 characters will be displayed. The type of alert box is determined by the numeric value of *<alert_type>*.

ALERT() will return TRUE if OK is clicked, and FALSE if Cancel is clicked.

SEE ALSO

DIALOG.BOX(), MESSAGE()

ALIGNMENT()

v: **ALL**

DIALOG BOX

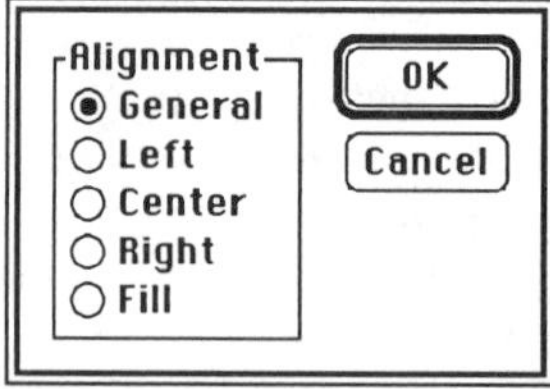

SYNTAX

ALIGNMENT(<*type*>)
ALIGNMENT?()

EQUIVALENT COMMAND

Format Alignment

USAGE

The ALIGNMENT() macro function sets the alignment for the selected cells. The allowed argument values correspond to the five radio buttons in the dialog box. Type 1, General, is the default and aligns text left, numbers right, and logical and error values centered. Type 5 alignment fills the cell with the first character of the string in the cell.

The ALIGNMENT?() macro function takes no argument, but shows the Format Alignment dialog box instead.

SEE ALSO

CELL(*"prefix"*,*<reference>*), BORDER(), CELL.PROTECTION(), FORMAT.NUMBER(), STYLE()

ARGUMENT()

***v:* ALL**

SYNTAX

ARGUMENT(*<argument_name>*,
[*<type>*][,*<storage_location>*])

EQUIVALENT COMMAND

None

USAGE

The ARGUMENT() macro function is used to define the interface to a function macro, which is like a callable subroutine that performs a specific calculation. The subroutine call consists of a reference or named reference, a left parenthesis, some arguments, and a right parenthesis (see **SUBROUTINE**). The first macro functions in a function macro are the ARGUMENT() functions, one for each argument, in order.

<argument_name> is the name given to an argument passed to a function macro, entered as a quoted string.

<type> represents the expected type(s) of the argument as a numeric code. The allowed codes are 1 (number), 2 (string), 4 (logical), 8 (reference), 16 (error), 64 (array). If an argument can be of more than one type, add the numbers that

correspond to the types you expect and use the sum for <*type*>. If it is omitted, 7 (1+2+4) is assumed.

<*storage_location*> is the location on the macro sheet to store the argument as a cell reference. If it is omitted, the value of the argument is stored as the definition of <*argument_name*>.

The ARGUMENT() functions are placed at the beginning of a function macro to define a name for each of its arguments. They can also test values passed to a function macro for type. If they are not of the correct type and cannot be converted, the function macro will not be calculated and will return with the error value #VALUE!.

The ARGUMENT() functions can also define a cell (or cells for an array) in which the arguments are to be stored on the macro sheet. If you include the <*storage_location*> reference, the reference will be set equal to the value of the argument as well as the <*argument_name*>. If you omit <*storage_location*>, only the name will be defined as equal to the value of the argument.

Note that some functions, such as INDEX(), HLOOKUP(), VLOOKUP(), and LOOKUP() will not work on an array as a defined value, but only on an array as a defined cell range.

If you do not include the <*storage_location*> argument, you must use the SET.NAME() macro function to change the value of an argument. If you do include the <*storage_location*> argument, you must use the SET.VALUE() macro function to change the value of the argument. In the second case, if you use the SET.NAME() macro function, you will redefine <*argument_name*> to equal a value instead of a reference to <*storage_location*>.

SEE ALSO

RETURN(), RESULT(), SUBROUTINE

BEEP()

v: ALL

SYNTAX

BEEP()

EQUIVALENT COMMAND

None

USAGE

The BEEP() macro function sounds the system beep. Use it to signal a user to do something, a dialog box, or the end of a macro. Use it also during debugging to signal when you reach different parts of a macro.

BORDER()

v: ALL

DIALOG BOX

Border
☐ Outline
☐ Left
☐ Right
☐ Top
☐ Bottom
OK
Cancel

SYNTAX

BORDER(<*outline*>,<*left*>,<*right*>,<*top*>,<*bottom*>)
BORDER?()

EQUIVALENT COMMAND

Format Border

USAGE

Setting the BORDER() macro function arguments TRUE is equivalent to checking the checkboxes in the dialog box and will cause the corresponding sides of the selected cells to have borders. As this is part of the formatting, clearing the formatting of a cell will clear the border styles.

The BORDER?() macro function takes no argument, but shows the Format Border dialog box instead.

<*outline*> is a flag to outline the cell selection. The allowed logical values are TRUE (outline) and FALSE (do not outline).

<*left*>, <*right*>, <*top*>, <*bottom*> are flags to put a border on the left, right, top, or bottom of each of the selected cells. The allowed values are TRUE (border) or FALSE (no border).

SEE ALSO

ALIGNMENT(), CELL.PROTECTION(), FORMAT.NUMBER(), STYLE()

BREAK()

v: 1.5

SYNTAX

BREAK()

EQUIVALENT COMMAND

None

USAGE

The BREAK() macro function interrupts the operation of a FOR()/NEXT() or a WHILE()/NEXT() loop, terminates the loop, and continues execution of the macro at the statement after the NEXT() macro function. This function is used primarily with the IF() function to terminate a loop prematurely.

SEE ALSO

FOR(), HALT(), NEXT(), WHILE()

CALCULATE.NOW()

v: **ALL**

SYNTAX

CALCULATE.NOW()

EQUIVALENT COMMAND

Options Calculate Now

USAGE

The CALCULATE.NOW() macro function recalculates any uncalculated cells on all open worksheets. It is needed only if manual recalculation has been set with the CALCULATION() macro function.

SEE ALSO

CALCULATION()

CALCULATION()

v: ALL

DIALOG BOX

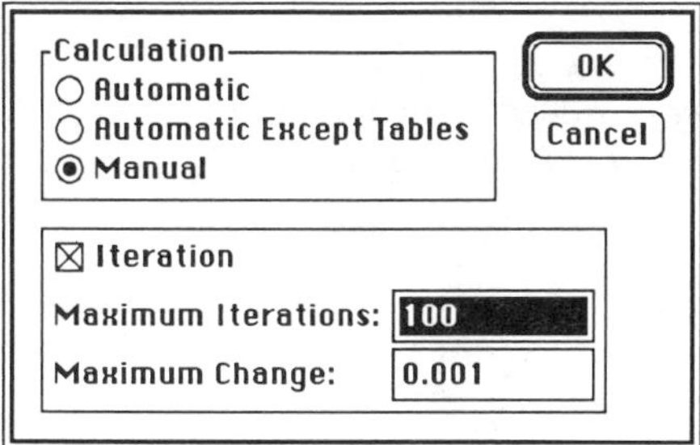

SYNTAX

CALCULATION(<*calculation_method*>,[<*iteration_flag*>], [<*maximum_iterations*>],[<*maximum_change*>]**)**
CALCULATION?()

EQUIVALENT COMMAND

Options Calculation

USAGE

With the CALCULATION() macro function, you can set manual or automatic calculation. You can also turn on worksheet iteration for iterative solutions of circular equations. For iteration, set the maximum number of iterations to try before giving up, and the maximum change in a cell to force continued iteration. Note that <*maximum_change*> is the absolute change in a value in a cell, not the fractional change of that value.

Enter <*calculation_method*> as a numeric code. The allowed values are 1 (automatic), 2 (automatic except tables), or 3 (manual).

<*iteration_flag*> is a flag to indicate iteration. The allowed logical values are TRUE (iterate) and FALSE (do not iterate). If it is omitted, the previous value is assumed.

<*maximum_iterations*> is the maximum number of times to iterate the spreadsheet, entered as an integer. If it is omitted, the previous value is assumed.

<*maximum_change*> is the maximum change in a value on the spreadsheet that will cause Excel to continue iterating, entered as a numeric value. If it is omitted, the previous value is assumed.

The CALCULATION?() macro function takes no argument, but shows the Options Calculation dialog box instead.

SEE ALSO

CALCULATE.NOW()

CALLER()

v: 1.5

SYNTAX

CALLER()

EQUIVALENT COMMAND

None

USAGE

The CALLER() macro function returns the cell reference of the cell or cells that called the currently running macro. The reference will be an absolute, external reference, containing the name of the calling sheet as well as the cell reference on that sheet. If the macro that contains this function was called by a reference in a worksheet cell, the address of that cell is returned. If the cell was part of an array formula, the range reference is returned instead of just the cell reference. If the macro containing the function was called with the Macro Run command or an Option–Command-Key combination, the function will return the error value #REF!.

CANCEL.COPY()

v: **1.5**

SYNTAX

CANCEL.COPY()

EQUIVALENT COMMAND

None

USAGE

The CANCEL.COPY() macro function is used with the COPY() macro command. When you use COPY(), the current selection is outlined with a marquee, marking it as the selection that has been copied. After you have pasted the selection, use CANCEL.COPY() to cancel the copy selection and turn off the marquee.

SEE ALSO

COPY()

CELL.PROTECTION()

v: **ALL**

DIALOG BOX

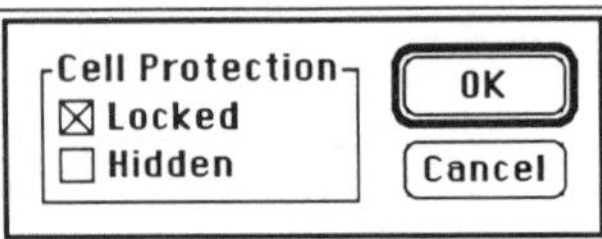

SYNTAX

CELL.PROTECTION(<*locked*>,<*hidden*>)
CELL.PROTECTION?()

EQUIVALENT COMMAND

Format Cell Protection

USAGE

Setting the CELL.PROTECTION() macro function arguments TRUE will cause the selected cells to be marked as locked or hidden. The default for all cells is locked, so this command is needed to unlock or hide cells. *<locked>* is a flag to lock the selected cells. The allowed logical values are TRUE (lock) and FALSE (do not lock). *<hidden>* is a flag to hide the selected cells. The allowed values are TRUE (hide) and FALSE (do not hide). Cell protection is not turned on until you execute the PROTECT.DOCUMENT() macro function or the Options Protect Document command. Protecting the cells makes it impossible to change the contents. Hiding the cells does not change the values shown, but makes invisible the formulas that produced the values.

The CELL.PROTECTION?() macro function takes no argument, but shows the Format Cell Protection dialog box instead.

SEE ALSO

ALIGNMENT(), BORDER(), FORMAT.NUMBER(), PROTECT.DOCUMENT(), STYLE(), UNLOCKED.NEXT/PREV(), CELL("protect",*<reference>*) worksheet function

CHANGE.LINK()

v: **1.04**

SYNTAX

CHANGE.LINK(<*old_document*>,<*new_document*>**)**
CHANGE.LINK?([<*old_document*>]**)**

EQUIVALENT COMMAND

File Links (Change button)

USAGE

The CHANGE.LINK() macro function is equivalent to pressing the Change button in the File Links command dialog box. If you move or change the name of a supporting document of a worksheet, you must use File Links to reestablish the connection between the worksheet and its supporting document. CHANGE.LINK() allows you to do that in a macro. The arguments are strings containing the old and new names of the supporting documents. Both names must contain the name of the file and directory to it. This can get complicated, especially given the long folder names sometimes used on the Macintosh.

You can get the old name from the contents of a cell that references a function on it. The function name will be prefaced with the complete reference to the document containing it. You can also use the LINKS() macro function, which will give you an array of all supporting documents, including their directories.

If you insist on writing your own directory paths, see the Introduction for more information.

The second form of the function, CHANGE.LINK?(), brings up the File Links dialog box for you to choose the old file names and the File Open dialog box for you to choose the new file name. If you include the *<old_ file_name>* argument, only the new file name dialog box will appear.

SEE ALSO

DIRECTORY(), DOCUMENTS(), FILES(), LINKS(), OPEN.LINKS()

CHECK.COMMAND()

v: **1.5**

SYNTAX

CHECK.COMMAND(*<bar_number>***,***<menu_position>***,** ***<command_position>***,***<check_flag>***)**

EQUIVALENT COMMAND

None

USAGE

The CHECK.COMMAND() macro function puts a check mark or removes it from in front of a command in a user-created menu. The check marks do not change the operation of a command on a menu; rather they are markers for indicating selected commands. Attempting to put check marks in front of any of the built-in commands on the built-in menu bars (see the ADD.BAR() macro function) will cause a macro error.

Enter <*bar_number*> as an integer. The allowed values are 1 through 21. Values 1 through 3 are for Excel's built-in menu bars. Values 4 through 6 are reserved for future versions. Values 7 through 21 are for custom menu bars defined with the ADD.BAR() macro function.

Enter <*menu_ position*> as either a string containing the menu name or the number of its position. The Apple menu is not counted.

<*command_ position*> represents the command on the menu to put a check mark after, entered as either a string containing the command name or the number of its position. Position numbers count from the top, with the first command as number 1. Horizontal bars used for command separators are also counted.

Enter <*check_ flag*> as a logical value. The allowed values are TRUE (check command) and FALSE (remove or do not check).

SEE ALSO

ADD.BAR(), ADD.COMMAND(), ADD.MENU(), DELETE.BAR(), DELETE.COMMAND(), DELETE.MENU(), ENABLE.COMMAND(), GET.BAR(), RENAME.COMMAND(), SHOW.BAR()

DIALOG BOX

Clear
All
Formats
Formulas
OK
Cancel

SYNTAX

CLEAR(<*component*>**)**
CLEAR?()

EQUIVALENT COMMAND

Edit Clear

USAGE

The CLEAR() macro function clears the current selection of cells of their formulas, formats or both. Its argument is a numeric code. The allowed values are 1 (all), 2 (formats), and 3 (formulas).

The CLEAR?() macro function takes no argument but shows the Edit Clear dialog box instead.

CLOSE()

v: **1.5**

SYNTAX

CLOSE([<*save_flag*>]**)**

EQUIVALENT COMMAND

None, but see below

USAGE

The CLOSE() macro function is equivalent to clicking on the close box in the corner of a window. Its argument is a flag indicating whether to save the document. The allowed values are TRUE (save) and FALSE (don't save). If it is omitted, a dialog box will ask you if you want to save any changes.

SEE ALSO

File Close All command, **OPEN()**, **OPEN.LINKS()**

COLUMN.WIDTH()

v: **ALL**

DIALOG BOX

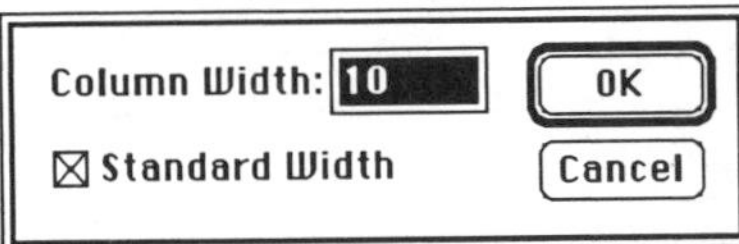

SYNTAX

COLUMN.WIDTH(<*width*>[,<*reference*>])
COLUMN.WIDTH?()

EQUIVALENT COMMAND

Format Column Width

USAGE

The COLUMN.WIDTH() macro function is also equivalent to dragging the boundaries of a column with the mouse.

The <*width*> argument is the width of a column in character widths. Fractional widths are allowed.

<*reference*> represents the columns to change the width of, expressed as an external cell reference, or a cell reference in the R1C1 style as a string. If the string is used, the active window is assumed. If it is omitted, the current selection is assumed.

The COLUMN.WIDTH?() macro function takes no argument but shows the Format Column Width dialog box instead. The Standard Width check box resets the width to the default (10 characters).

COMBINATION()

v: ALL

DIALOG BOX

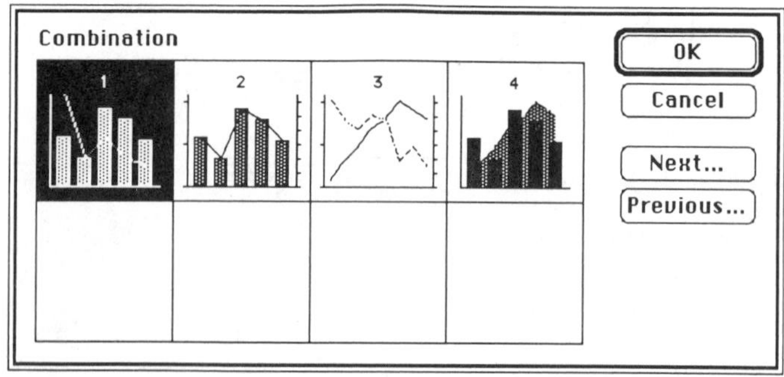

SYNTAX

COMBINATION(<*chart_type*>)
COMBINATION?()

EQUIVALENT COMMAND

Gallery Combination

USAGE

When you execute the COMBINATION() macro function, the current chart will become a combination chart with its data series split between the two chart types. The <*chart_type*> corresponds to one of the numbers at the top of each chart type in the Gallery Combination dialog box.

The COMBINATION?() macro function takes no argument but shows the Gallery Combination dialog box instead.

The Next and Previous buttons cycle through the different chart types on the Gallery menu.

SEE ALSO

GALLERY.*xxxx*()

COPY()

***v:* ALL**

SYNTAX

COPY()

COMMAND EQUIVALENT

Edit Copy

USAGE

When the COPY() macro function is executed, it marks the current selection for copying by outlining it with a marquee.

After you have pasted the selection, use the CANCEL.COPY() macro function to cancel the copy selection and turn off the marquee.

SEE ALSO

CANCEL.COPY(), COPY.CHART(), COPY.PICTURE(), CUT(), FILL.DOWN()/RIGHT(), PASTE(), PASTE.SPECIAL(), SELECT()

COPY.CHART()

v: **ALL**

DIALOG BOX

Copy Chart to Clipboard
- (•) As Shown on Screen
- ( ) As Shown when Printed

OK
Cancel

SYNTAX

COPY.CHART(<*size*>)
COPY.CHART?()

EQUIVALENT COMMAND

Edit Copy Chart

USAGE

When the COPY.CHART() macro function is executed, a copy of the current chart, as a picture, is put onto the clipboard for use in other applications. The value of the argument corresponds to the two radio buttons on the dialog box. If <*size*> equals 1, a copy of the chart as shown on the screen is made. When printing, Excel normally expands the size of a chart to fill the printed page. If <*size*> equals 2, a copy of the chart as it would appear when printed would be made.

The COPY.CHART?() macro function takes no argument but shows the Edit Copy Chart dialog box instead.

To copy the chart as values, axis settings, labels, and so forth, to use in creating another chart in Excel, use the COPY() function.

SEE ALSO

COPY(), COPY.PICTURE(), CUT(), PASTE(), PASTE.SPECIAL()

COPY.PICTURE()

***v:* ALL**

SYNTAX

COPY.PICTURE()

EQUIVALENT COMMAND

Edit Copy Picture when a worksheet or macro sheet is active. This command is obtained by holding the Shift key down when selecting the Edit Copy command.

USAGE

The COPY.PICTURE() macro function puts a copy of the current selection, as a picture, on the clipboard for use in other applications. The copied selection will include row and column headings. You can copy sections of a worksheet to the clipboard using this function but must use the COPY.-CHART() macro function to copy a chart as a picture.

To copy the selection as values, instead of as a picture, use the COPY() macro function.

SEE ALSO

COPY(), COPY.CHART(), CUT(), PASTE(), PASTE.SPECIAL()

CREATE.NAMES()

v: **ALL**

DIALOG BOX

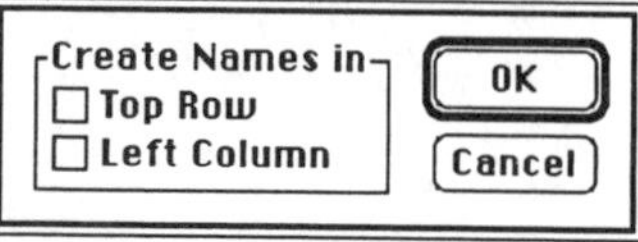

SYNTAX

CREATE.NAMES(*<top_row>*,*<left_column>*)
CREATE.NAMES?()

EQUIVALENT COMMAND

Formula Create Names

USAGE

The CREATE.NAMES() macro function is used to name cells using text above them, to their right, or both. Select the cells to be named and the cells containing the names before executing this function. If any cell on the name rows or columns does not contain a string, it will not be used to create a name.

Each argument is a flag that corresponds to one of the check boxes in the dialog box. The check boxes determine what portion of the slection to use to name the cells in the rest of the selection. The allowed values are TRUE and FALSE.

The CREATE.NAMES?() macro function takes no argument, but shows the Formula Create Names dialog box instead.

To see the current definitions, look in the Formula Define Name dialog box.

SEE ALSO

DEFINE.NAME(), DELETE.NAME(), GET.DEF(), GET.NAME()

CUT()

v: **ALL**

SYNTAX

CUT()

EQUIVALENT COMMAND

Edit Cut

USAGE

When you execute the CUT() macro function, the current selection is marked for cutting by outlining it with a marquee. Use the PASTE() macro function to insert the selection elsewhere. The selection will be copied to the clipboard if necessary. If you do not paste the selection elsewhere in Excel, it will not be removed from its current location. Use the CLEAR() macro function to delete the contents of cells, or the EDIT.DELETE() macro function to remove the cells and shift the other cells up or left to fill the hole.

SEE ALSO

CLEAR(), COPY(), COPY.CHART(), COPY.PICTURE(), EDIT.DELETE(), PASTE(), PASTE.SPECIAL()

DATA.DELETE()

v: **1.5**

SYNTAX

DATA.DELETE()
DATA.DELETE?()

EQUIVALENT COMMAND

Data Delete

USAGE

When the DATA.DELETE() macro function is executed, it will select records in the current database according to the selection criteria. Records that match the criteria will be removed, and all others will be moved up. See the Introduction for more information on databases.

The DATA.DELETE?() macro function brings up a dialog box with a warning that deleting the records is permanent and cannot be undone with the Edit Undo command. You may cancel the command at this point.

SEE ALSO

DATA.FIND(), DATA.FIND.NEXT(), DATA.FIND.PREV(), EXTRACT(), SET.CRITERIA(), SET.DATABASE()

DATA.FIND()

v: **ALL**

SYNTAX

DATA.FIND(<*find_or_exit*>)
DATA.FIND.NEXT()
DATA.FIND.PREV()

EQUIVALENT COMMAND

Data Find or **Data Exit Find**, depending on argument

USAGE

The DATA.FIND() macro function argument is a flag to find or to exit the Data Find command. The allowed logical values are TRUE (execute Data Find) and FALSE (execute Data Exit Find). When it is executed with the argument TRUE, DATA.FIND() searches the current database for the first record that matches the current criteria and highlights it. The scroll bars change and scroll the highlight along records that match the criteria. To access the next matching record, execute the DATA.FIND(TRUE) macro function again, or execute the DATA.FIND.NEXT() macro function. To access the previously highlighted record, execute the DATA.FIND.PREV() macro function.

To operate, a database range and criteria range must be defined with the Data Set Database and Data Set Criteria commands. See the Introduction for more information about databases and criteria.

Exit the Data Find command by editing a cell in the database, selecting a cell out of the database range, or executing the DATA.FIND(FALSE) function.

SEE ALSO

DATA.DELETE(), EXTRACT(), SET.CRITERIA(), SET.DATABASE()

DATA.SERIES()

v: ALL

DIALOG BOX

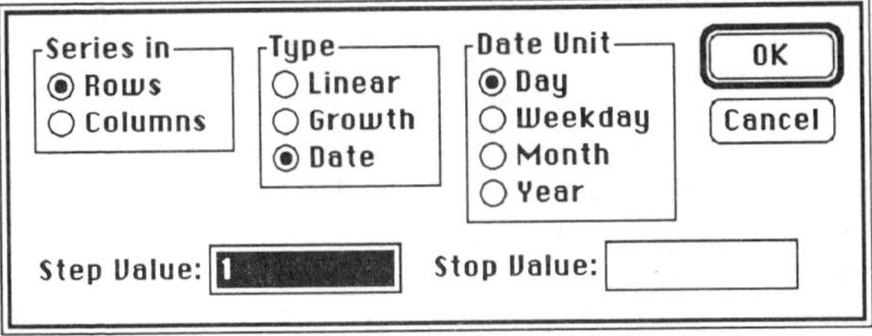

SYNTAX

DATA.SERIES(<*rows_columns*>[,<*type*>][,<*date_unit*>][,<*step*>][,<*stop*>])
DATA.SERIES?()

EQUIVALENT COMMAND

Data Series

USAGE

The DATA.SERIES() macro function fills the current selection with a sequence of numbers or dates. The starting value of the sequence is the number contained in the top row for series in columns or the left column for series in rows. In a linear series, the next value in the series is determined by adding *<step>* to the current value. In a growth series, the next value in the series is determined by multiplying the current value by *<step>*. A date series produces a series of dates that increment according to the *<date_unit>* and *<step>*. For all series, cells are filled until the end of the selection or the number *<stop>* is reached.

<rows_columns> is the direction to insert the series, and is equivalent to the Series in radio buttons. The allowed values are 1 (rows), or 2 (columns).

<type> is equivalent to the Type radio buttons, and represents the type of series to insert. The allowed values are 1 (linear), 2 (growth), and 3 (date). If it is omitted, 1 is assumed.

<date_unit> is equivalent to the Date Unit radio button, which determines the unit to use if *<type>* is 3 (date) or the Date radio button is selected. The allowed values are 1 (day), 2 (weekday), 3 (month), or 4 (year).

<step> is the increment between the numbers in the series. It is equivalent to the Step Value edit box. If it is omitted, 1 is assumed.

<stop> is the stop value for the series. It is equivalent to the Stop Value edit box. If it is omitted, the series will end when the selection is filled.

The DATA.SERIES?() macro function takes no argument, but shows the Data Series dialog box instead.

DEFINE.NAME()

***v:* ALL**

DIALOG BOX

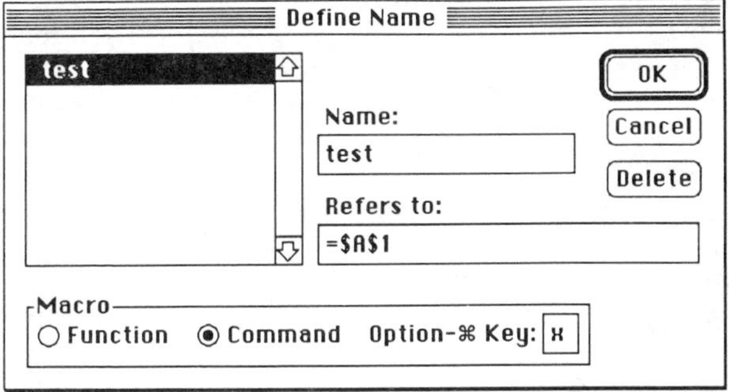

SYNTAX

DEFINE.NAME(<*name*>,[<*definition*>]
[,<*macro_type*>[,<*macro_key*>]])
DEFINE.NAME?()

EQUIVALENT COMMAND

Formula Define Name

USAGE

The most common use of the DEFINE.NAME() macro function is to define a symbolic name for a cell reference. However, it can also define a name for a number, a string, a logical value, or an array. If the definition is a reference on a macro sheet, you can also set the macro type and invocation key. This is where you define command and function macros. The dialog box shown is for a macro reference. A worksheet reference lacks the macro box at the bottom of the dialog box.

Enter <*name*> as a string. It must be a legal Excel name. A legal Excel name starts with a letter and can contain letters, numbers, the period, or underscore, but no spaces.

<*definition*> is equivalent to the Refers to: edit box, and can be a reference, number, string, logical value, or formula, to define as <*name*>. If it is a formula, it must be a string with references in the R1C1 style. If it is omitted, the reference of the current selection is assumed.

Enter the <*macro_type*> for a reference on a macro sheet as a numeric code. The allowed values are 1 (function macro) or 2 (command macro).

<*macro_key*> is the keyboard key to invoke a command macro when pressed with Command and Option. Enter it as a one-character string. It is ignored if <*macro_type*> is not 2.

The DEFINE.NAME?() macro function takes no argument but shows the Formula Define Name dialog box instead.

To see a list of the current definitions, select the Formula Define Name command and select the definition you are interested in. Quit the command with Cancel, so you do not change any of your definitions. You can get the name that goes with a definition with the GET.DEF() macro function, or get the definition that goes with a name with the GET.-NAME() macro function.

SEE ALSO

CREATE.NAMES(), DELETE.NAME(), GET.DEF(), GET.NAME(), SET.NAME()

DELETE.BAR()

v: **1.5**

SYNTAX

DELETE.BAR(<*bar_number*>**)**

EQUIVALENT COMMAND

None

USAGE

The DELETE.BAR() macro function deletes from memory a custom menu bar created with the ADD.BAR() macro function. It cannot be the currently displayed menu bar. To delete the currently displayed menu bar, first put up a different menu bar with the SHOW.BAR() macro function, then delete the custom menu bar.

Enter <*bar_number*> as an integer. The allowed values are 7 through 21. You cannot delete the built-in menu bars 1 through 3, and you cannot delete the currently displayed bar.

SEE ALSO

ADD.BAR(), ADD.COMMAND(), ADD.MENU(), CHECK.COMMAND(), DELETE.COMMAND(), DELETE.MENU(), ENABLE.COMMAND(), GET.BAR(), RENAME.COMMAND(), SHOW.BAR()

DELETE.COMMAND()

v: **1.5**

SYNTAX

DELETE.COMMAND(*<bar_number>*,*<menu_position>*, *<command_position>***)**

EQUIVALENT COMMAND

None

USAGE

The DELETE.COMMAND() macro function deletes a custom command from a menu. Any commands below the deleted one will be moved up, and their command position will decrease by one. If the command does not exist, the macro function will return the error value #VALUE! and halt the macro; otherwise it will return the logical value TRUE. You cannot delete any of the built-in menus.

Enter *<bar_number>* as an integer. The allowed values are 1 through 3 and 7 through 21. Values 1 through 3 are for Excel's built-in menu bars. Values 4 through 6 are reserved for future versions. Values 7 through 21 are for custom menu bars defined with the ADD.BAR() macro function.

Enter *<menu_position>* as either a string containing the menu name or the number of its position. Position numbers count from the left with the first menu as number 1. The Apple menu is not counted.

Enter *<command_position>* as either a string containing the command name or the number of its position. Position numbers count from the top with the first command as number 1.

Horizontal bars used for command separators are also counted.

SEE ALSO

ADD.BAR(), ADD.COMMAND(), ADD.MENU(), CHECK.COMMAND(), DELETE.BAR(), DELETE.MENU(), ENABLE.COMMAND(), GET.BAR(), RENAME.COMMAND(), SHOW.BAR()

DELETE.FORMAT()

v: **ALL**

SYNTAX

DELETE.FORMAT(<*format_string*>**)**

EQUIVALENT COMMAND

Format Number/Delete

USAGE

With the DELETE.FORMAT() macro function, you can only delete custom number formats that you have created with the Format Number command. You cannot delete any of Excel's built-in formats. See FORMAT.NUMBER for more information on formats and format syntax.

Enter the format to delete as a string.

SEE ALSO

FORMAT.NUMBER()

DELETE.MENU()

v: 1.5

SYNTAX

DELETE.MENU(*<bar_number>***,***<menu_position>***)**

EQUIVALENT COMMAND

None

USAGE

The DELETE.MENU() macro function deletes a custom menu from a menu bar. You cannot delete any of Excel's built-in menus. Any menus to the right of the deleted menu will be moved to the left, and their menu position will decrease by one. If the menu does not exist, the macro function will return the error value #VALUE! and halt the macro; otherwise, it will return the logical value TRUE.

Enter *<bar_number>*, the menu bar from which to delete the menu, as an integer. The allowed values are 1 through 3 and 7 through 21. Values 1 through 3 are for Excel's built-in menu bars. Values 4 through 6 are reserved for future versions. Values 7 through 21 are for custom menu bars defined with the ADD.BAR() macro function.

Enter *<menu_position>*, the menu on the menu bar to delete, as either a string containing the menu name or the number of its position. Position numbers count from the left with the first menu as number 1. The Apple menu is not counted. Only custom menus created with the ADD.MENU() macro function can be deleted.

SEE ALSO

ADD.BAR(), ADD.COMMAND(), ADD.MENU(), CHECK.COMMAND(), DELETE.BAR(), DELETE.COMMAND(), ENABLE.COMMAND(), GET.BAR(), RENAME.COMMAND(), SHOW.BAR()

DELETE.NAME()

***v:* ALL**

SYNTAX

DELETE.NAME(<*name_string*>)

EQUIVALENT COMMAND

Formula Define Name, (Delete button)

USAGE

The DELETE.NAME() macro function deletes a formula name from the list of name definitions.

Enter the argument as a string containing the name to delete.

SEE ALSO

CREATE.NAMES(), DEFINE.NAME(), GET.DEF(), GET.NAME(), SET.NAME()

DEREF()

v: **ALL**

SYNTAX

DEREF(<*reference*>**)**

EQUIVALENT COMMAND

None

USAGE

The DEREF() macro function returns the contents of <*reference*>. This function is needed only in those functions that do not evaluate a reference before using it, such as the SET.NAME() macro function.

SEE ALSO

REFTEXT(), TEXTREF()

DIALOG.BOX()

v: 1.5

SYNTAX

DIALOG.BOX(<*dialog_reference*>**)**

EQUIVALENT COMMAND

None

USAGE

The DIALOG.BOX() macro function displays a dialog box and returns a user's selections in that box. If the user clicks the OK button, the function will return TRUE, and the Input/Output column of the dialog definition table will contain the user's selections in the dialog box. If the user clicks the Cancel button, the function will return FALSE. Using the DIALOG.BOX() macro function on the following dialog definition table:

Macro2

	A	B	C	D	E	F	G	H	I
1	=DIALOG.BOX(Dialog_Box)								
2	=RETURN()								
3									
4	Description	Item	Horiz	Vert	Item	Item	Item Text	Input/Output	Table for
5		Number	Pos	Pos	Heigth	Width		Values	list box
6	Dialog Box Outline:		97	54	362	223			One
7	Static Text:	5	27	13			A Sample Dialog Box:		Two
8	OK Button (default):	1	275	20	64		OK		Three
9	Cancel Button:	2	275	60	64		Cancel		Four
10	Icon:	17	212	46			2		Five
11	Group Definition:	11	211	109	142	65	Group	1	Six
12	Option Button:	12	219	128			Option Button 1		Seven
13	Option Button:	12	219	146			Option Button 2		Eight
14	Edit Box:	6	14	47	171				Nine
15	Combination Edit Box:	6	14	79	171				Ten
16	Combination List Box:	16	15	112	171	92	R[-10]C[2]:R[-1]C[2]	1	
17	Check Box:	13	224	184			Check Box	FALSE	
18									
19									

produces the following dialog box:

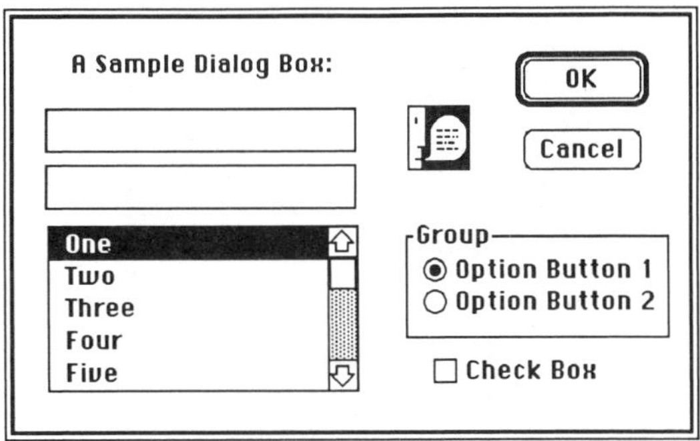

Each item in the dialog box is described with one line in the dialog definition table, including the dialog box itself. The dialog definition table consists of seven columns and at least two rows. The table shown here is in cells B6:H17. The text in column A and rows 4 and 5 is descriptive only. The table of values in column I is for the List item. The first row in the dialog definition table describes the outline and location of the dialog box itself. The rest of the rows of the table describe the different items in the dialog box.

The first column (B) contains the item number, which determines the type of the item:

ITEM TYPE	DESCRIPTION
1	Default OK Button
2	Cancel Button
3	OK Button
4	Default Cancel Button
5	Static Text
6	Text Edit Box
7	Integer Edit Box
8	Number Edit Box

ITEM TYPE	DESCRIPTION
9	Formula Edit Box
10	Reference Edit Box
11	Option Button Group
12	Option Button
13	Check Box
14	Group Box
15	List Box
16	Combination List/Text Edit Box
17	Icon

Columns 2 through 5 contain the location of the upper-left corner of the item as well as the height and width of the item. The location and size are in screen units, with the origin in the upper-left corner of the screen. Screen units are in points, which are 1/72 inch. If you leave these columns blank, Excel will automatically place and size all of your dialog items.

Column 6 contains text strings needed by some of the items, such as the text of a Static Text item or the title of a Group item. Of special note is the text for the dialog box itself, which not only gives it a title, but changes the dialog box to an active dialog box. An active dialog box can be moved, and values and references can be inserted by clicking on cells in sheets outside of the dialog box. A static dialog box cannot be moved, and only items in it can be accessed. Also of special note is the item text of a list item, which is the name or cell reference (in the R1C1 style) of the contents of the list (for example, Row 16).

Column 7 is for input and output items. Input items are the initial contents of edit items and the selections of groups of buttons. Outputs are the final values of the buttons and boxes in the dialog box when OK is pressed. If Cancel is pressed, the contents of this column are not changed.

You can also create a dialog box graphically with the Dialog Editor included with Excel. After you have created it, you can copy it and then paste the dialog definition table into a worksheet.

SEE ALSO

ALERT(), INPUT(), MESSAGE()

DIRECTORY()

v: **1.5**

SYNTAX

DIRECTORY([<*path_string*>]**)**

EQUIVALENT COMMAND

None

USAGE

The DIRECTORY() macro function sets and returns the current directory. See the Introduction for the syntax of a directory path. Enter the path to the new current directory as a quoted string. If it is omitted, the path to the current directory is returned. See the Introduction for more information about directory paths.

SEE ALSO

DOCUMENTS(), LINKS(), WINDOWS()

DISPLAY()

v: **ALL**

DIALOG BOX

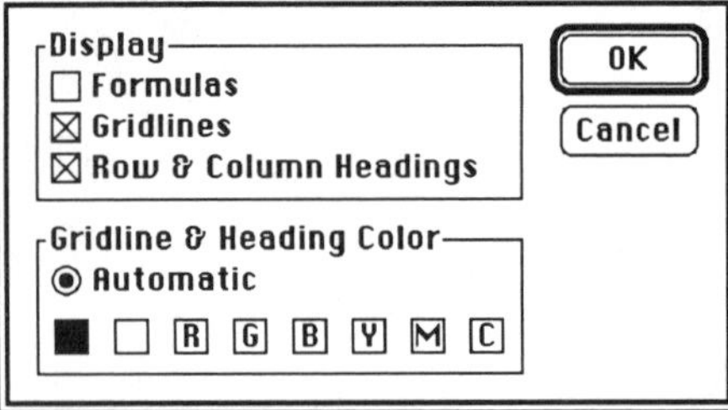

SYNTAX

DISPLAY(*<formulas>***,***<gridlines>***,***<headings>***,**
<zeroes>,***<line_color>***)**
DISPLAY?()

EQUIVALENT COMMAND

Options Display

USAGE

With the DISPLAY() macro function, you can set how worksheets and macro sheets are displayed on the monitor. This does not affect how they are printed. The first three arguments are equivalent to the check boxes in the dialog box.

<formulas> is a flag to show formulas or values of cells. The allowed values are TRUE (show formulas) or FALSE (show values).

<gridlines> is a flag to show the grid lines. The allowed values are TRUE (show gridlines) or FALSE (do not show gridlines).

<headings> is a flag to show the row and column headings. The allowed values are TRUE (show headings) and FALSE (do not show headings).

<zeroes> is a flag to show cells containing the number 0 as a number or as a blank. It is present only for compatability with PC Excel and is ignored here. The allowed values are TRUE (show as numbers) and FALSE (show as blanks).

<line color> represents the color to use for gridlines and headings, entered as a numeric code. The allowed values are 0 (automatic), 1 (black), 2 (white), 3 (red), 4 (green), 5 (blue), 6 (yellow), 7 (magenta), and 8 (cyan).

Note that the *<gridlines>* and *<headings>* settings apply only to the display of the sheet on the monitor and not to the printed sheet. Set the *<gridlines>* and *<headings>* options for printing with the File Page Setup command.

The DISPLAY?() macro function takes no argument, but shows the Options Display dialog box instead.

SEE ALSO

PAGE.SETUP(), SHOW.INFO()

DOCUMENTS()

v: ALL

SYNTAX

DOCUMENTS()

EQUIVALENT COMMAND

None

USAGE

The DOCUMENTS() macro function returns a horizontal array of strings containing all of the currently open documents on the desktop. Documents will be displayed in the list in the order in which they were opened or created. Use the INDEX() function to select a particular document name from the list.

SEE ALSO

DIRECTORY(), LINKS(), WINDOWS()

ECHO()

v: ALL

SYNTAX

ECHO(<*screen_updating*>**)**

EQUIVALENT COMMAND

None

USAGE

The ECHO() macro function turns screen updating on or off. A slow macro or spreadsheet calculation can be speeded up significantly if screen updating is turned off while the macro is calculating. Screen updating is automatically turned back on when a macro ends.

The argument is a flag to turn on or off screen updating. The allowed values are TRUE (update the screen continuously) and FALSE (do not update the screen).

EDIT.DELETE()

v: **ALL**

DIALOG BOX

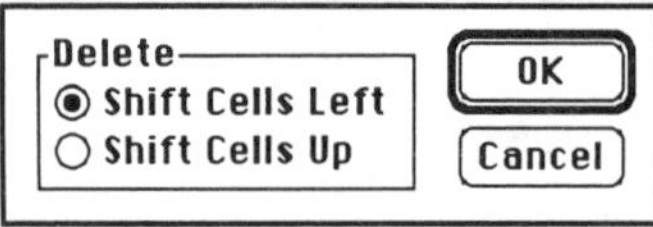

SYNTAX

EDIT.DELETE(*<shift_direction>***)**
EDIT.DELETE?()

EQUIVALENT COMMAND

Edit Delete

USAGE

Executing the EDIT.DELETE() macro function deletes the current selection of cells. After the cells are deleted, the argument determines how the remaining cells are moved to fill in for the deleted cells. The allowed values are 1 (shift cells left) and 2 (shift cells up). Use the CLEAR(1) macro function to simply erase the contents of some cells without moving those around them. Note that the current selection need not be a complete row or column.

The EDIT.DELETE?() macro function takes no argument but shows the Edit Delete dialog box instead.

SEE ALSO

CLEAR(), CUT(), INSERT(), PASTE()

ENABLE.COMMAND()

v: **1.5**

SYNTAX

ENABLE.COMMAND(*<bar_number>***,***<menu_position>***,** *<command_position>***,***<enable_flag>***)**

EQUIVALENT COMMAND

None

USAGE

The ENABLE.COMMAND() macro function enables or disables a command in a user created menu. Disabled commands are grayed out and cannot be selected. Attempting to enable or disable any of the built-in commands on the built-in menu bars (see the ADD.BAR() macro function) will cause a macro error.

Enter the menu *<bar_number>* as an integer. The allowed values are 1 through 3 and 7 through 21. Values 1 through 3 are for Excel's built-in menu bars. Values 4 through 6 are reserved for future versions. Values 7 through 21 are for custom menu bars defined with the ADD.BAR() macro function.

<menu_position> represents the menu on the menu bar, entered as either a string containing the menu name or the number of its position. Position numbers count from the left

with the first menu as number 1. The Apple menu is not counted.

<command_position> is the command on the menu to enable or disable, entered as either a string containing the command name or the number of its position. Position numbers count from the top with the first command as number 1. Horizontal bars used for command separators are also counted. If you use the number 0, the whole menu is enabled or disabled.

<enable_flag> enables or disables the command. The allowed values are TRUE (enable) and FALSE (disable).

SEE ALSO

ADD.BAR(), ADD.COMMAND(), ADD.MENU(), CHECK.COMMAND(), DELETE.BAR(), DELETE.COMMAND(), DELETE.MENU(), GET.BAR(), RENAME.COMMAND(), SHOW.BAR()

ERROR()

v: **ALL**

SYNTAX

ERROR(*<error_flag>***,[***<error_macro>***])**

EQUIVALENT COMMAND

None

USAGE

The ERROR() macro function enables error trapping during macro execution. If error trapping is enabled and an error is encountered, execution will branch to the top of <*error_macro*>. If you omitted <*error_macro*>, the macro error dialog box shown below will be displayed, giving you the chance to halt the macro, step through the macro one step at a time, or continue. This is the default condition, which you get without executing the ERROR() macro function.

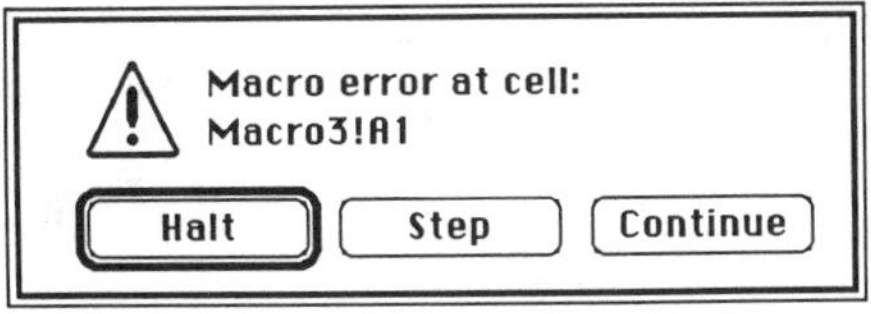

If error checking is disabled, your macro will ignore errors and continue execution. Be sure you really want to ignore error checking before you disable it.

<*error_flag*> turns on or off error checking. The allowed values are TRUE (check for errors) and FALSE (ignore errors).

<*error_macro*> is a cell reference to a macro to execute if an error is detected. If it is omitted, the macro error dialog box will be displayed.

EXTRACT()

v: **ALL**

DIALOG BOX

Extract

☐ Unique Records Only

OK

Cancel

SYNTAX

EXTRACT(<*unique_records*>**)**
EXTRACT?()

EQUIVALENT COMMAND

Data Extract

USAGE

The EXTRACT() macro function is equivalent to the Data Extract command. The current database is searched for records that match the current criteria. Copies of the requested fields of the matching records are placed in the output range. The output range must be selected before executing EXTRACT(). The argument is equivalent to the check box in the dialog box, which is a flag to suppress insertion of matching records in the output range. If the argument is TRUE, only one copy of each matching record is copied to the output range, even if that record matches more than one row of your criteria range. Also, if the part you are extracting is the same in two records, only one will be copied to the output range. If it is FALSE, all matches to the criteria will be extracted, possibly resulting in identical records in the output range. See the Introduction for information about databases.

The EXTRACT?() macro function takes no argument, but shows the Data Extract dialog box instead.

SEE ALSO

DATA.DELETE(), DATA.FIND(), DATA.FIND.NEXT(), DATA.FIND.PREV(), SET.CRITERIA(), SET.DATABASE()

FILE.DELETE()

v: **ALL**

DIALOG BOX

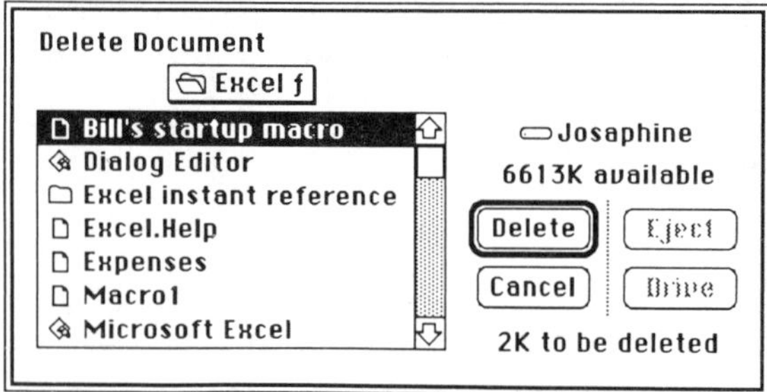

SYNTAX

FILE.DELETE(<*file_name*>**)**
FILE.DELETE?()

EQUIVALENT COMMAND

File Delete

USAGE

When the FILE.DELETE() macro function is executed, Excel attempts to delete the specified file from the current disk and directory. If the file is not in the current directory, Excel will display a dialog box, which requests you to locate the file for it. You can use the DIRECTORY() macro function to change the current directory and the FILES() macro function to get a list of the files in a directory. Enter <*file_name*> as a string. The File Delete dialog box does not close when you delete a file, but stays open for you to delete additional files. Close it with the cancel button.

The FILE.DELETE?() macro function takes no argument, but shows the File Delete dialog box instead.

SEE ALSO

DIRECTORY(), FILES()

FILES()

v: **1.5**

SYNTAX

FILES(<*path_string*>**)**

EQUIVALENT COMMAND

None

USAGE

The FILES() macro function lists the files in a directory as a horizontal array. Since it results in an array, it must be entered into a row of cells while holding down the Command key. The file names will fill the array of cells from the left. Any unused cells will be set to the error value #N/A.

The argument is a path to a directory or file. See the section on directory paths in the Introduction for the syntax of a path.

If it is omitted, the current directory and the Wildcard * is assumed. You could also use the DIRECTORY() macro function to change the current directory. After the last colon, enter the file name you want to list or use the wildcards * and ? to list several files. The wildcard ? matches any single character and * matches anything. If your path ends in a filename instead of a directory, the function will return the filename, if it exists, or #N/A if it does not.

SEE ALSO

DIRECTORY()

FILL.DOWN() /RIGHT()

v: ALL

SYNTAX

FILL.DOWN()
FILL.RIGHT()

EQUIVALENT COMMAND

None

USAGE

The FILL.DOWN() macro function copies the cells along the top of the current selection and pastes them into the cells below them in the rest of the selection.

The FILL.RIGHT() macro function copies the cells along the left side of the current selection and pastes them into the cells to their left in the rest of the selection.

SEE ALSO

COPY(), PASTE(), PASTE.SPECIAL()

FONT()

v: **ALL**

DIALOG BOX

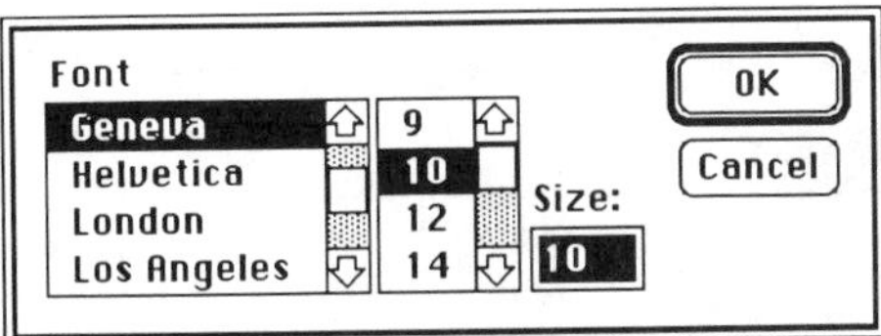

SYNTAX

FONT(<*font_name*>,<*font_size*>**)**
FONT?()

EQUIVALENT COMMAND

Options Font

USAGE

The FONT() macro function is used to set the font and size for the row and column headings, and for the cell contents of the active sheet.

Enter *<font_name>* as a string. The allowed values are the font names that are installed on your system. Differences in capitalization are ignored when comparing *<font_name>* with the names of the installed fonts.

Enter *<font_size>* as a number in points. A point is 1/72 inch.

The FONT?() macro function takes no argument, but shows the Options Font dialog box instead.

SEE ALSO

STYLE()

FOR()

***v:* 1.5**

SYNTAX

FOR(*<counter_name>***,***<start>***,***<stop>***,***<step>***)**

EQUIVALENT COMMAND

None

USAGE

The FOR() macro function controls the start of a FOR()/NEXT() loop. The FOR() macro function first defines a variable named *<counter_name>* and sets it equal to the number *<start>*. Execution begins by comparing the value of *<counter_name>* with *<stop>*. If *<counter_name>* is less than or equal to *<stop>*, the statements between FOR() and NEXT() are executed once. On reaching the NEXT() statement, the value of *<counter_name>* is incremented by *<step>*, and execution begins again. If *<counter_name>* is greater than *<stop>*, execution continues with the statement after NEXT().

Note that *<counter_name>* is the name of the counter, not the cell reference of the storage location. If you use a cell reference for *<counter_name>*, Excel will try to use the contents of that cell as a name for the loop counter. If you name a cell *<counter_name>* with the Format Define Name command, the FOR() macro function will redefine that name to equal the value of the loop counter instead of the cell reference. If you need a cell to contain the value of the loop counter, use a SET.VALUE() macro function, after the FOR() macro function, to set the value of the cell to the value of *<counter_name>*.

SEE ALSO

BREAK(), WHILE()

FORMAT.NUMBER()

v: ALL

DIALOG BOX

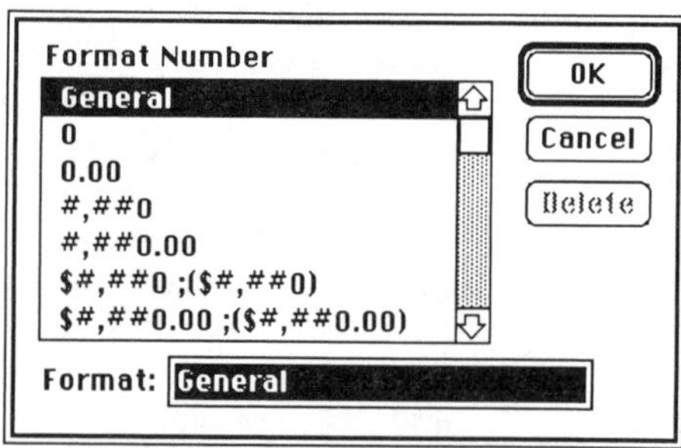

SYNTAX

FORMAT.NUMBER(<*format_string*>)
FORMAT.NUMBER?()

EQUIVALENT COMMAND

Format Number

USAGE

The FORMAT.NUMBER() macro function sets the format for numbers in the selected cells. Enter the argument as a string.

The FORMAT.NUMBER?() macro function takes no argument, but shows the Format Number dialog box instead.

The Format Number command is used to set the format and color of the contents of a cell. You can select a built-in format or create a custom format. Any custom formats you create will appear in the list box in the dialog box, so that you can apply them elsewhere on a worksheet. The Delete button deletes a custom format from the list of formats. The Format Number list box shows all of the built-in and custom formats. Selected formats are displayed in the Format edit box. Insert the format to apply to the selected cells in the Format edit box. Select a format from the list or type in a custom format.

The built-in formats are shown below. The code shown is that returned by the CELL() function.

FORMAT	CODE
General	G
0	F0
0.00	F2
#,##0	F0
#,##0.00	F2
$#,##0;($#,##0)	C0
$#,##0.00;($#,##0.00)	C2
0%	P0
0.00%	P2
0.00E+00	S2
m/d/yy	D4
d-mmm-yy	D1
d-mmm	D2
mmm-yy	D3
h:mm AM/PM	D7
h:mm:ss AM/PM	D6
h:mm	D9
h:mm:ss	D8
m/d/yy h:mm	D4

A format consists of four parts separated by semicolons. The first part is the format for positive numbers, the second is for negative numbers, the third is for zero numbers, and the last is for text strings. You can omit any of the sections. If there are only three sections, they are interpreted as the three number formats. If there are two sections, the first is for positive and zero numbers, and the second is for negative numbers. If there is only one section, it applies to all numbers. If you want to use a number format with omitted sections and include a text format, insert an @ symbol after the last semicolon. If you have repeated semicolons, with no format between them, those types of numbers will not be displayed.

A format within each section consists of two parts, the number format and the color. The number format consists of symbols to define where the characters of the number will go.

SYMBOL	EFFECT
0	Marks positions that will always contain a character, and marks the number of digits to round to on the right side of the number. If the number does not have enough characters on the left or right of the decimal, the zeros will be displayed.
#	Marks the positions of characters and rounding on the right side of the number.
.	Marks the position of the decimal point to determine rounding.
%	Multiplies the number by 100 and puts a percent sign on the right.
,	Inserts a comma every three digits.

SYMBOL	EFFECT
E–,e–,E+,e+	Prints the number in scientific notation. E– and e– cause a minus sign to be placed before a negative exponent, and nothing before a positive exponent. E+ and e+ cause a minus sign to be placed before a negative exponent and a plus sign to be placed in front of a positive exponent.
:$–+() space	Displays the character in the position indicated. To display other characters, precede them with a backslash (\) or put them in double quotes ("").
\c	Displays the character c.
*c	Repeats the character c to fill out the column.
"string"	Displays the string between the quotes.
@	Text in the cell will be inserted here.

The color is appended to the number format as a string enclosed in square brackets. The string contains the name of the color. The allowed values are [BLACK], [WHITE], [RED], [GREEN], [BLUE], [YELLOW], [MAGENTA], and [CYAN].

Cells can also be formatted as dates and times. A date is stored as a *serial day number*. A *serial day number* is the date expressed as the number of days from Jan. 1, 1904. The time is expressed as a fractional part of a day. The date and time formats are

SYMBOL	DESCRIPTION
m	The month as a number with no leading zeros, or the minute if it is immediately after the h symbol.
mm	The month as a number with a leading zero for values less than 10, or the minute if it is immediately after the *h* symbol.

SYMBOL	DESCRIPTION
mmm	The month as a three-character abbreviation.
mmmm	The full name of the month.
d	The day as a number with no leading zeros.
dd	The day as a number with a leading zero for values less than 10.
ddd	The day of the week as a three-character abbreviation.
dddd	The full name of the day of the week.
yy	The year as a two-digit number.
yyyy	The year as a four-digit number.
h	The hour as a number with no leading zeros.
hh	The hour as a number with a leading zero for values less than 10.
m	The minute as a number with no leading zeros, or the month if it is not immediately after the *h* symbol.
mm	The minute as a number with a leading zero for values less than 10, or the month if it is not immediately after the *h* symbol.
s	The second as a number with no leading zeros.
ss	The second as a number with a leading zero for values less than 10.
AM/PM am/pm A/P a/p	Display time using the 12-hour clock; otherwise use a 24-hour clock.

SEE ALSO

ALIGNMENT(), CELL("prefix",*<reference>*), **BORDER()**, **CELL.PROTECTION()**, **STYLE()**

FORMULA()

v: **ALL**

SYNTAX

FORMULA(*<formula_string>*[,*<reference>*]**)**

EQUIVALENT COMMAND

None

USAGE

The FORMULA() macro function inserts a formula or value into a cell just as if you had typed it there directly. The argument *<formula_string>* is a string, containing a formula, the text representation of a number, string, or logical value. Any references in a formula must be in the R1C1 style. See the **A1/R1C1** command for more information about the R1C1 style. *<reference>* (available in Version 1.5 or later) is the location to insert the formula, entered as a cell reference. If it is omitted, the active cell is used. If the reference is an array of cells, only the upper-left corner is used. This function, and the FORMULA.ARRAY() and the FORMULA.FILL() macro functions are the primary way for a command macro to put values into a worksheet cell.

If the active document is a chart, this function inserts or replaces a data series or text label, depending on the contents of *<formula_string>* and on the selected object (if any) on the chart. The rules are exactly the same as when you select a chart object and type into the edit bar.

SEE ALSO

FORMULA.ARRAY(), FORMULA.FILL(), SET.NAME(), SET.VALUE()

FORMULA.ARRAY()

v: **ALL**

SYNTAX

FORMULA.ARRAY(*<formula_string>***[,***<reference>***])**

EQUIVALENT COMMAND

None

USAGE

The FORMULA.ARRAY() macro function inserts an array formula or value into a range of cells, as if you had entered it there while holding down the Command key. The argument *<formula_string>* is a string containing a formula, the text representation of a number, string, or logical value. Any references in a formula must be in the R1C1 style. See the **A1/R1C1** command for more information about the R1C1 style.

<reference> (available in Version 1.5 or later) is the location to insert the formula, entered as a cell reference. If it is omitted, the active cell is used.

SEE ALSO

FORMULA(), FORMULA.FILL(), SET.NAME(), SET.VALUE()

FORMULA.FILL()

v: **ALL**

SYNTAX

FORMULA.FILL(*<formula_string>*[,*<reference>*]**)**

EQUIVALENT COMMAND

None

USAGE

The FORMULA.FILL() macro function inserts a formula or value into a range of cells just as if you had entered it there while holding down the Option key. The argument *<formula_string>* is a string containing a formula, the text representation of a number, string, or logical value. Any references in a formula must be in the R1C1 style. See **A1/R1C1** for more information about the R1C1 style. *<reference>* (available in Version 1.5 or later) is the location to insert the formula, as a cell reference. If it is omitted, the active cells are used.

SEE ALSO

FORMULA(), FORMULA.ARRAY(), SET.NAME(), SET.VALUE()

FORMULA.FIND.[*xxxx*]

***v:* ALL**

DIALOG BOX

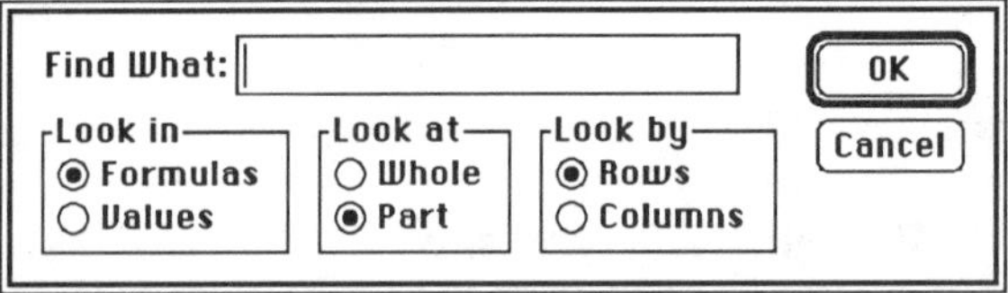

SYNTAX

FORMULA.FIND(<*find_what*>**,**<*look_in*>**,**<*look_at*>**,**
<*look_by*>[,<*direction*>]**)**
FORMULA.FIND?()
FORMULA.FIND.NEXT()
FORMULA.FIND.PREV()

EQUIVALENT COMMAND

Formula Find

USAGE

These functions search a macro or a worksheet for a string or number. The FORMULA.FIND() arguments are equivalent to the options in the dialog box. *<find_what>* represents the value to search for. Enter it as a string. If it is not found, the function returns FALSE. You can use the * and ? wildcards to search for parts of a value. The ? wildcard stands for any single character and * stands for any number of characters.

The *<look_in>* argument indicates where to look. Enter it as a numeric code. The allowed values are 1 (in formulas) and 2 (in values). The *<look_at>* argument indicates how much of the value to match. Enter it as a numeric code. The allowed values are 1 (whole entry) and 2 (partial entry). Setting *<look_at>* equal to 2 (part) is equivalent to putting the * wildcard on both sides of *<find_what>*. The *<look_by>* argument indicates how to search, entered as a numeric code. The allowed values are 1 (by rows) and 2 (by columns). This function is probably most useful for searching for error values such as #NUM! or #VALUE.

The FORMULA.FIND?() macro function takes no argument, but shows the Formula Find dialog box instead. Holding down the Shift key when pressing the OK button is equivalent to *<direction>*=2 (match previous).

The FORMULA.FIND.NEXT(), and FORMULA.FIND.-PREV() macro functions are equivalent to executing FORMULA.FIND() again with all the arguments the same as the last time it was called, except for *<direction>*. In the first case, *<direction>* = 1 and in the next, *<direction>* = 2.

SEE ALSO

FORMULA.GOTO()

FORMULA.GOTO()

v: ALL

DIALOG BOX

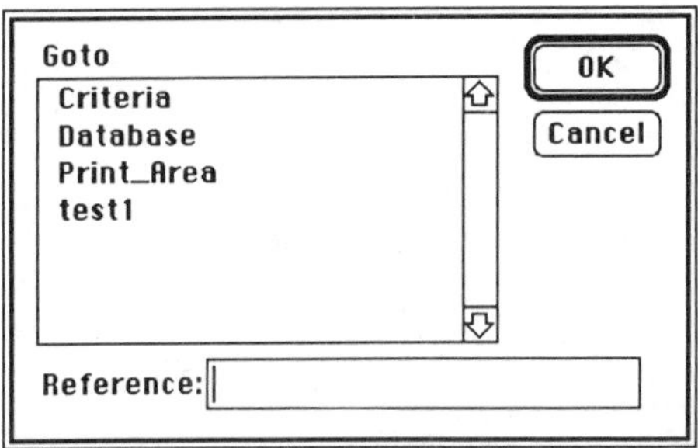

SYNTAX

FORMULA.GOTO(<*reference*>)
FORMULA.GOTO?()

EQUIVALENT COMMAND

Formula Goto

USAGE

The FORMULA.GOTO() macro function is similar in function to the SELECT() macro function without its second argument. Use it to select a cell or range of cells and scroll the worksheet or macro sheet until they are in view. This is most useful for locating named ranges. Enter the argument as a cell reference or a string containing a cell reference in the R1C1 style.

The FORMULA.GOTO?() macro function takes no argument, but shows the Formula Goto dialog box instead. The user would then select from the list in the dialog box, or type an alternate selection.

The dialog box shows the currently defined ranges. Select a named range or type the reference into the edit box.

SEE ALSO

SELECT()

FREEZE.PANES()

v: **1.5**

SYNTAX

FREEZE.PANES([<*freeze_or_unfreeze*>]**)**

EQUIVALENT COMMAND

Options Freeze Panes

USAGE

The FREEZE.PANES() macro function freezes or unfreezes the titles in the active sheet. The allowed argument values are TRUE (freeze the panes) and FALSE (unfreeze the panes). If the argument is omitted, the function will toggle from one to the other.

To make titles stay motionless while you scroll through a sheet, use the split bar or the SPLIT() macro function to split the sheet horizontally, vertically, or both. You may then scroll one pane while the others remain motionless. However, all of the panes have their own scroll bars, and can be scrolled. The FREEZE.PANES() function locks the upper and left panes, depending on how the current window is split, and removes their scroll bars so that they cannot be moved. Only the lower-right corner of the sheet can be scrolled. Attempting to execute FREEZE.PANES() on a sheet that has not been split will cause an error.

SEE ALSO

SPLIT()

FULL()

v: ALL

SYNTAX

FULL(<*expand_window*>**)**

EQUIVALENT COMMAND

None, but see below

USAGE

The FULL() macro function is equivalent to double-clicking the title bar of a window or clicking the zoom box on the title bar. The argument is a flag to expand the window to full size or contract it to normal size. If the argument is TRUE, the window will be expanded as much as possible. If the argument is FALSE, the window will be returned to its original size. If you omit the argument, the function will set as a toggle; that is, the size of the window will alternate every time you execute the function.

SEE ALSO

SIZE()

GALLERY.*xxxx*()

***v:* 1.5**

DIALOG BOX

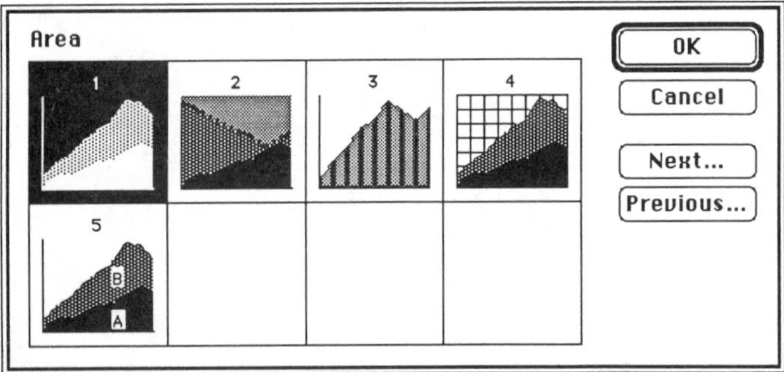

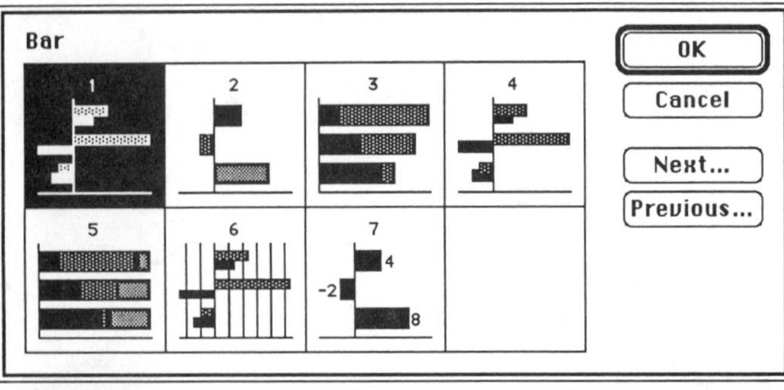

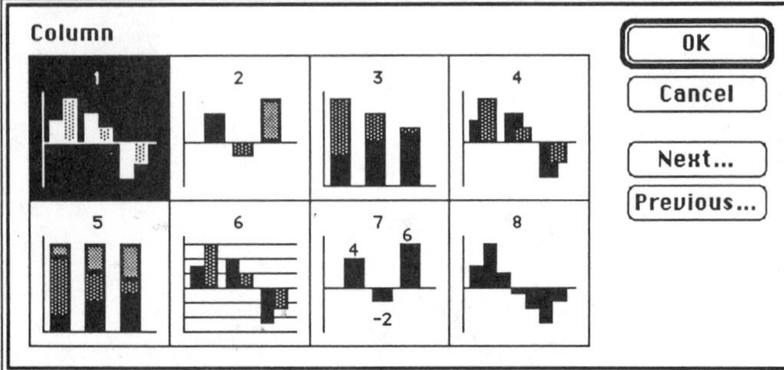

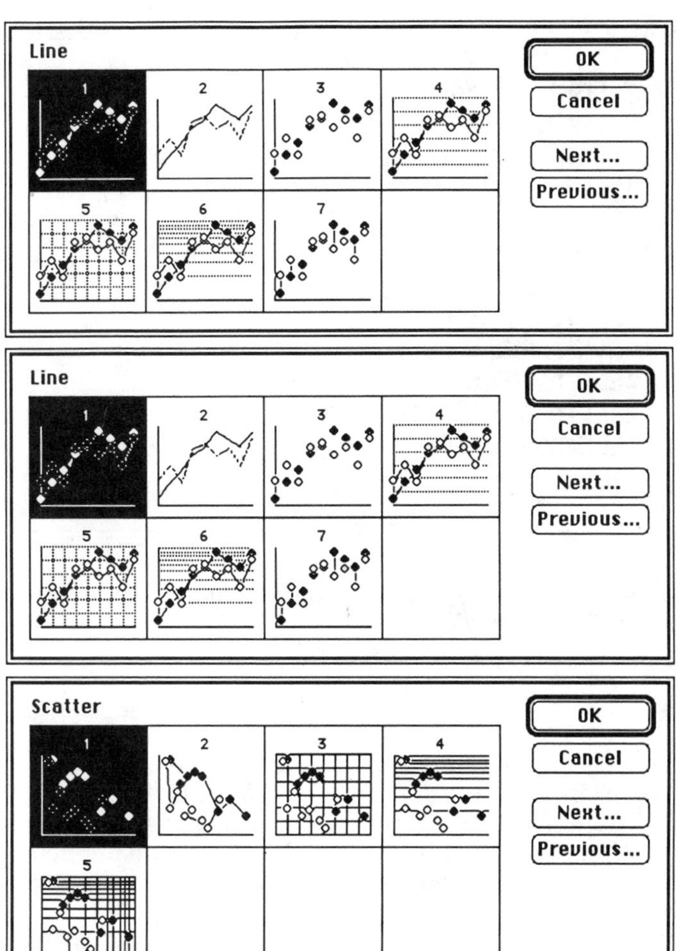
Line
1
2
3
4
5
6
7
OK
Cancel
Next...
Previous...
Line
1
2
3
4
5
6
7
OK
Cancel
Next...
Previous...
Scatter
1
2
3
4
5
OK
Cancel
Next...
Previous...

SYNTAX

GALLERY.AREA(<*type*>)
GALLERY.AREA?()
GALLERY.BAR(<*type*>)
GALLERY.BAR?()
GALLERY.COLUMN(<*type*>)
GALLERY.COLUMN?()
GALLERY.LINE(<*type*>)
GALLERY.LINE?()
GALLERY.PIE(<*type*>)
GALLERY.PIE?()
GALLERY.SCATTER(<*type*>)
GALLERY.SCATTER?()

EQUIVALENT COMMAND

Gallery Area, Gallery Bar, Gallery Column, Gallery Line, Gallery Pie, Gallery Scatter

USAGE

The GALLERY.????() functions set the type and format of the active chart from a list of predefined formats. While all of the chart formats can be set with other commands, these commands set all of the options with a single command or function. The Next and Previous buttons cycle to the next or previous Gallery command.

The GALLERY.AREA() Area command selects area charts. The <*type*> arguments are integer numbers that select one of the formats in the equivalent dialog box. The number at the top of each format in the dialog box is the one to use for *type*.

The GALLERY.BAR() macro function selects horizontal bar charts.

The GALLERY.COLUMN() macro function which selects vertical bar charts.

The GALLERY.LINE() macro function selects line charts.

The GALLERY.PIE() macro function selects pie charts.

The GALLERY.SCATTER() macro function selects scatter charts.

The COMMAND?() forms of the Gallery macro functions take no arguments, but show the Gallery dialog boxes instead.

SEE ALSO

COMBINATION()

GET.BAR()

v: **1.5**

SYNTAX

GET.BAR()

EQUIVALENT COMMAND

None

USAGE

The GET.BAR() macro function returns the bar number of the active menu bar. See the **ADD.BAR()** macro function for more information about menu bars.

SEE ALSO

ADD.BAR(), ADD.COMMAND(), ADD.MENU(), CHECK.COMMAND(), DELETE.BAR(), DELETE.COMMAND(), DELETE.MENU(), ENABLE.COMMAND(), RENAME.COMMAND(), SHOW.BAR()

GET.CELL()

v: **1.5**

SYNTAX

GET.CELL(*<information_to_get>***,[***<reference>***])**

EQUIVALENT COMMAND

None

USAGE

The GET.CELL() macro function is used to get information about a cell. It combines the capabilities of the CELL(), COLUMN(), ROW(), and TYPE() functions. If the *<reference>* range contains more than one cell, the cell in the upper-left corner is used. If it is omitted, the upper-left cell in the current selection is assumed. The following list shows what GET.CELL() will return for different values of *<information_to_get>*.

VALUE	RESULT
1	The cell's reference as text in R1C1 style.
2	The cell's row number.
3	The cell's column number, where column A is 1, B is 2, and so forth.
4	The type of value contained in the cell as a numeric code: 1 (number), 2 (text), 4 (logical value), 16 (error value), and 64 (array).
5	The value contained in the cell.
6	The formula contained in the cell as text.
7	The number format of the cell as text.
8	The alignment of the value in the cell as a numeric code: 1 (general), 2 (left), 3 (center), 4 (right), or 5 (fill).
9	TRUE if the cell has a left border; otherwise FALSE.
10	TRUE if the cell has a right border; otherwise FALSE.
11	TRUE if the cell has a top border; otherwise FALSE.
12	TRUE if the cell has a bottom border; otherwise FALSE.
14	TRUE if the cell is locked; otherwise FALSE.
15	TRUE if the cell is hidden; otherwise FALSE.
16	The column width of the cell measured in character widths.
17	The height of the cell in points (1/72 of an inch).
18	The name of the font used in the cell as text.
19	The font size in points (1/72 of an inch).

VALUE	RESULT
20	TRUE if the text in the cell is bold, otherwise FALSE.
21	TRUE if the text in the cell is italic, otherwise FALSE.

SEE ALSO

CELL(), COLUMN(), GET.FORMULA(), ROW(), TEXTREF(), TYPE()

GET.DEF()

v: **1.5**

SYNTAX

GET.DEF(<*definition_string*>[,<*document_name*>])

EQUIVALENT COMMAND

None

USAGE

The GET.DEF() macro function searches the list of definitions in the document <*document_name*> for a match with <*definition_string*>. If a match is found, the name associated with this definition is returned. Only the first matching definition will be returned. If the definition contains a reference, it will be in the R1C1 style, no matter how it was originally defined. If

<document_name> is omitted, the macro sheet containing the GET.DEF() macro function is assumed.

To see the currently defined names in a document, select it and execute the Formula Define name command. Quit the command with the Cancel button.

SEE ALSO

CREATE.NAMES(), DEFINE.NAME(), DELETE.NAME(), GET.NAME(), SET.NAME()

GET.DOCUMENT

v: **1.5**

SYNTAX

GET.DOCUMENT(*<information_to_get>*[,*<document_name>*])

EQUIVALENT COMMAND

None

USAGE

The GET.DOCUMENT() macro function gets information about an open document. The following list shows what GET.DOCUMENT() will return for different values of *<information_to_get>*. Information that returns an array must be entered in an appropriate number of cells while holding down the Command key. If <*document_name*> is omitted, the active document is assumed.

VALUE	RESULT
1	The document's name as a string.
2	The document's directory as a string or #N/A if it has not yet been saved.
3	The document's type as a numeric code: 1 (worksheet), 2 (chart), or 3 (macro sheet).
4	TRUE if changes have been made in the document since the last time it was saved, otherwise FALSE.
5	TRUE if the document was opened *read only*, otherwise FALSE.
7	TRUE if the document's contents are protected, otherwise FALSE.
9	If the document is a worksheet or macro sheet, the first row number. It will return 0 if the document is empty or 1 if the document is not empty. If the document is a chart, the chart type as a numeric code: 1 (area), 2 (bar), 3 (column), 4 (line), 5 (pie), or 6 (scatter).
10	If the document is a worksheet or macro sheet, the number of the last row used. If the document is empty, it returns 0. If the document is a chart, the chart type of the overlay chart as a numeric code: 1 (area), 2 (bar), 3 (column), 4 (line), 5 (pie), or 6 (scatter). If there is no overlay chart, it returns #N/A.
11	If the document is a worksheet or macro sheet, the number of the first column. If the document is empty, it returns 0; otherwise it returns 1. If the document is a chart, the number of series of data on the main chart.

VALUE	RESULT
12	If the document is a worksheet or macro sheet, the number of the last column used. If the document is empty, it returns 0. If the document is a chart, the number of series of data on the overlay chart.
13	The number of open windows.
14	The state of calculation as a numeric code: 1 (automatic), 2 (automatic except tables), 3 (manual).
15	TRUE if iteration is enabled, otherwise FALSE.
16	The maximum number of iterations to do before stopping.
17	The smallest change that will trigger another iteration.
19	TRUE if *precision as displayed* is set, otherwise FALSE.

SEE ALSO

GET.WINDOW(), GET.WORKSPACE()

GET.FORMULA()

v: **ALL**

SYNTAX

GET.FORMULA(<*reference*>)

EQUIVALENT COMMAND

None

USAGE

The GET.FORMULA() macro function gets the contents of the upper-left cell in <*reference*> and returns it in a string as it would appear in the formula bar. Any references in the formula will be converted to R1C1 format. <*reference*> must be a specific external reference (for example, "Worksheet 1!A1"), a nonspecific external reference to the active document (for example, "!A1") will not work.

SEE ALSO

CELL(), COLUMN(), GET.CELL(), ROW(), TEXTREF(), TYPE()

GET.NAME()

v: **ALL**

SYNTAX

GET.NAME(<*name_string*>**)**

EQUIVALENT COMMAND

None

USAGE

The GET.NAME() macro function searches the list of defined names for one that matches the argument, and then returns its definition as a string. References contained in the returned string will be in the R1C1 style. If only a name is used, the list of defined names in the macro sheet containing the function is searched. You can include an external reference to the active document, or to any other open document with the name.

SEE ALSO

CREATE.NAMES(), DEFINE.NAME(), DELETE.NAME(), GET.DEF(), SET.NAME()

GET.WINDOW()

v: **1.5**

SYNTAX

GET.WINDOW(<*information_to_get*>
[,<*window_name*>])

EQUIVALENT COMMAND

None

USAGE

The GET.WINDOW() macro function gets information about an open window. The following list shows what GET.WINDOW()

will return for different <*information_to_get*> values. Note that values 13–16 Enter these values in an appropriate number of cells while holding down the Command key. If <*window_name*> is omitted, the active window is assumed.

VALUE	RESULT
1	The window's name as a string.
2	The number of the window, for cases of multiple windows into the same document created with the Window New Window command.
3	The *x* position, in points, of the upper-left corner of the window measured from the upper-left corner of the screen. One point equals 1/72 inch.
4	The *y* position, in points, of the upper-left corner of the window measured from the upper-left corner of the screen.
5	The width of the window in points.
6	The height of the window in points.
8	TRUE if formulas are displayed, FALSE otherwise.
9	TRUE if gridlines are displayed, FALSE otherwise.
10	TRUE if column headings are displayed, FALSE otherwise.
12	The color of the gridlines and headings as a numeric code: 0 (automatic), 1 (black), 2 (white), 3 (red), 4 (green), 5 (blue), 6 (yellow), 7 (magenta), or 8 (cyan).
13	The number of the leftmost displayed column, in columns and fractions of a column, for each pane of a window as a one, two, or four element horizontal array.

VALUE	RESULT
14	The number of the topmost displayed row, in rows and fractions of a row, for each pane of a window as a one, two, or four element horizontal array.
15	The number of the rightmost displayed column in columns and fractions of a column, for each pane of a window as a one, two, or four element horizontal array.
16	The number of the bottom-most displayed row, in rows and fractions of a row, for each pane of a window as a one, two, or four element horizontal array.

SEE ALSO

GET.DOCUMENT(), GET.WORKSPACE(), SPLIT()

GET.WORKSPACE()

v: **1.5**

SYNTAX

GET.WORKSPACE(<*information_to_get*>)

EQUIVALENT COMMAND

None

USAGE

The GET.WORKSPACE() macro function gets information about the current operating environment. The following list shows what GET.WORKSPACE() will return for different values of <*information_to_get* >.

VALUE	RESULT
1	The name of the environment as a string, such as "Macintosh".
2	The version of Excel as a string, such as "1.5".
4	TRUE if the current referencing mode is R1C1 or FALSE if it is A1.
10	The current special mode as a numeric code: 0 (normal), 1 (data find), 2 (copy), or 3 (cut).
13	The usable width of the desktop in points.
14	The usable height of the desktop in points.
16	The amount of free memory in K bytes. A K byte is 1024 bytes.
17	The total memory in K bytes.
18	TRUE if there is a math coprocessor present, otherwise FALSE.

SEE ALSO

GET.DOCUMENT(), GET.WINDOW()

GOTO()

v: ALL

SYNTAX

GOTO(<*reference*>**)**

EQUIVALENT COMMAND

None

USAGE

The GOTO() macro function causes a branch of the currently running macro to the top-left cell of <*reference*>, which may be an external reference. This is a one-way branch, so encountering a RETURN() macro function will not bring you back here. To be able to branch and return, use the ref() macro function (see **SUBROUTINES**).

SEE ALSO

SUBROUTINES

HALT()

v: **1.5**

SYNTAX

HALT()

EQUIVALENT COMMAND

None

USAGE

The HALT() macro function halts the currently running macro and returns control to the desktop. It is most often used to stop a macro in cases of errors.

SEE ALSO

RETURN()

HLINE/PAGE/SCROLL()

v: ALL

SYNTAX

HLINE(<*lines*>)
HPAGE(<*pages*>)
HSCROLL(<*column_number*>,<*scroll_how*>)

EQUIVALENT COMMAND

None

USAGE

The HLINE() macro function causes the active pane in the active window to be scrolled horizontally by the number of columns specified in the argument. Negative values scroll to the left.

The HPAGE() macro function causes the active pane of the active window to be scrolled horizontally by the number of pages full of columns specified by the argument.

<*lines*> and <*pages*> are the number of lines or pages to scroll. Negative values scroll to the left.

The HSCROLL() macro function scrolls the active pane of the active window to a specific column, or to a column that is a certain fraction of the way across the sheet. Worksheets and macro sheets are 256 columns wide.

<*column_number*> represents the column number to scroll to, or the fraction of the sheet to scroll across, depending on the value of <*scroll_how*>. The <*scroll_how*> argument is only available in Version 1.5. If <*scroll_how*> is TRUE, it is the column to scroll to, as an integer. If <*scroll_how*> is FALSE, it

is the fraction, in the range 0 to 1, of the worksheet to scroll across, where a value of 0 is column 1, and 1 is column 256. (If <*scroll_how*> is omitted, FALSE is assumed.)

SEE ALSO

VLINE/PAGE/SCROLL()

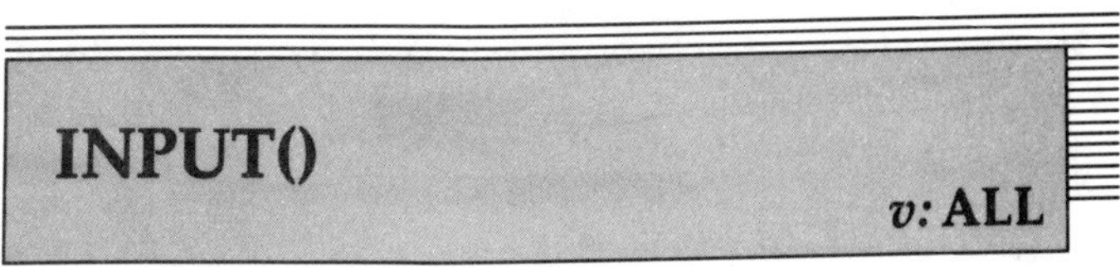

DIALOG BOX

The title string

This is the prompt string

OK

Cancel

SYNTAX

INPUT(<*prompt_string*>**,**<*input_type*>**,**[<*title_string*>]**)**

EQUIVALENT COMMAND

None

USAGE

The INPUT() macro function is used to get data from the user of a macro. When executed, it will bring up the dialog box shown, with a title <*title_string*> and a prompt message <*prompt_string*>. The prompt can be 84 characters long and the title 40 characters. If the title is omitted, "Input" is assumed. The user will type his input into an edit box, and Excel will attempt to convert it to the type specified by the code <*input_type*>. The allowed values are 0 (formula), 1 (number), ogical), 8 (reference), 16 (error), and 64 (array). If t make the conversion, it will put up an alert box with that message, and then return you to the edit box. If you want to allow multiple types of input, add together the codes for all of the types that you want. The INPUT() macro function will return a number for *<input_type>* 1, a logical for *<input_type>* 4, and strings for all of the others. Any references or formulas in the input will be converted to the R1C1 format. If the cancel button is pressed, the function will return FALSE.

When the dialog box is active, it can be moved, and you can select cells on a sheet to input references.

SEE ALSO

ALERT(), DIALOG.BOX()

INSERT()

v: **ALL**

DIALOG BOX

Insert
Shift Cells Right
Shift Cells Down
OK
Cancel

SYNTAX

INSERT(*<shift_direction>***)**
INSERT?()

EQUIVALENT COMMAND

Edit Insert

USAGE

Depending on the value of <*shift_direction*>, the INSERT() macro function moves the currently selected cells out of the way either by moving right all the cells to their right (a value of 1), or moving down all the cells below them (a value of 2). The space left by moving the cells is then filled with blank cells. This function is often used to insert new rows or columns into a document.

The INSERT?() macro function takes no argument, but shows the Edit Insert dialog box instead.

Be careful that your insertion does not damage some other part of your document. Unless you are certain that shifting the cells down or right will not damage some other part of your document, a safer way to move cells out of the way is to use the CUT() and PASTE() macro functions.

SEE ALSO

CLEAR(), CUT(), EDIT.DELETE(), PASTE()

LEGEND()

v: **ALL**

SYNTAX

LEGEND([*<add_or_delete>*])

EQUIVALENT COMMAND

Chart Add Legend, Chart Delete Legend

USAGE

When the LEGEND() macro function is executed, a legend will be either added to or deleted from the current chart, depending on the value of the argument. TRUE adds a legend, FALSE deletes one. If *<add_or_delete>* is omitted, LEGEND() acts as a toggle. A chart must be the current document when this command is executed or an error will result.

SEE ALSO

Format Legend... command, **Format Text** command, **PATTERNS()**

LINKS()

v: **ALL**

SYNTAX

LINKS(<*document_name*>**)**

EQUIVALENT COMMAND

None

USAGE

The LINKS() macro function returns a horizontal array of strings that contain the names and directory path of the dependent documents to the document named in the argument. If <*document_name*> is omitted, the active document is assumed. To see more than the first entry in the list, enter this command into a horizontal array of cells while holding down the Command key. You can also use the INDEX() function to select any single element in the list. If there are no links to a document, the command will return #N/A. This command can be used with the OPEN.LINKS() macro function to open all of the dependent documents.

SEE ALSO

DIRECTORY(), DOCUMENTS(), OPEN.LINKS(), WINDOWS()

MAIN.CHART.TYPE()

v: **ALL**

DIALOG BOX

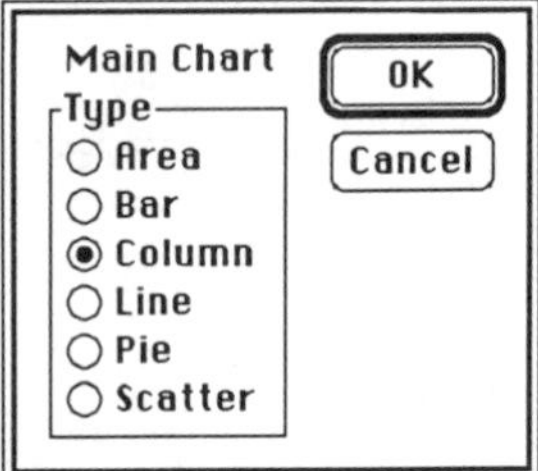

SYNTAX

MAIN.CHART.TYPE(<*chart_type*>)
MAIN.CHART.TYPE?()

EQUIVALENT COMMAND

Chart Main Chart Type

USAGE

Use the MAIN.CHART.TYPE() macro function to set the type of the main chart of the currently active chart. Excel allows you to split your data between two overlaid, semi-independent charts: the main chart and the overlay chart. See the Format Main Chart command for more information on main and overlay charts. The value of the argument is a numeric code that corresponds to selecting a radio button in the dialog box. The allowed values are 1 (area chart), 2 (bar chart), 3 (column chart), 4 (line chart), 5 (pie chart), and 6 (scatter chart).

SEE ALSO

GALLERY.xxxx(), OVERLAY.CHART.TYPE(), Format Main/Overlay Chart... command

MESSAGE()

v: **ALL**

SYNTAX

MESSAGE([<*on_or_off*>],[<*message_string*>]**)**

EQUIVALENT COMMAND

None

USAGE

The MESSAGE() macro function puts up a message line just below the menu bar. This is useful in long macros to tell the user what is going on.

Enter <*on_or_off*>, a flag to put up or take down the message line, as a logical value. The allowed values are TRUE (put up the message line) and FALSE (take down the message line). If it is omitted, the last value used is assumed.

Enter the message to display as a string. If it is omitted, a blank message is assumed.

SEE ALSO

ALERT(), DIALOG.BOX()

MOVE()

v: **ALL**

SYNTAX

MOVE(<*x_position*>,<*y_position*>,[<*window_name*>]**)**

EQUIVALENT COMMAND

None, but see below.

USAGE

The MOVE() macro function is equivalent to dragging the window by the title bar. The upper-left corner of the window is located to the right and down from the intersection of the left side of the screen and the bottom of the formula bar, according to <*x_position*> and <*y_position*>. These represent the *x,y* location of the final upper-left corner of the window, in points, entered as an integer. A point is 1/72 inch. Enter the name of the window to move as a string. If the name is omitted, the active window is assumed.

SEE ALSO

FULL(), SIZE()

NEW()

v: **ALL**

DIALOG BOX

New
Worksheet
Chart
Macro Sheet
OK
Cancel

SYNTAX

NEW([<*sheet_type*>])
NEW?()

EQUIVALENT COMMAND

File New

USAGE

Depending on the argument, the NEW() macro function creates a new (blank) worksheet (a value of 1), a macro sheet (2), or a chart (3). If it is omitted, a sheet of the same type as the active document is assumed.

The NEW?() macro function takes no argument, but shows the File New dialog box instead.

SEE ALSO

NEW.WINDOW()

NEW.WINDOW()

v: ALL

SYNTAX

NEW.WINDOW()

EQUIVALENT COMMAND

Window New Window

USAGE

The NEW.WINDOW() macro function creates a new window into the active worksheet or macro sheet.

SEE ALSO

NEW()

NEXT()

v: 1.5

SYNTAX

NEXT()

EQUIVALENT COMMAND

None

USAGE

The NEXT() macro function marks the end of a loop started with the FOR() or WHILE() macro function.

SEE ALSO

BREAK(), FOR(), WHILE()

OFFSET()

v: **ALL**

SYNTAX

OFFSET(<*reference*>,< *row_offset*>,< *column_offset*>)

EQUIVALENT COMMAND

None

USAGE

The OFFSET() macro function returns a reference of the same size and shape as <*reference*>, but offset from it by <*row_offset*> rows and <*column_offset*> columns. These represent the distance, in rows and columns, to offset the new reference from <*reference*>. Positive values offset down and to the right. Negative values offset up and to the left. The new reference must be on the sheet, or the function will return the error value #REF!.

SEE ALSO

RELREF()

OPEN()

v: ALL

DIALOG BOX

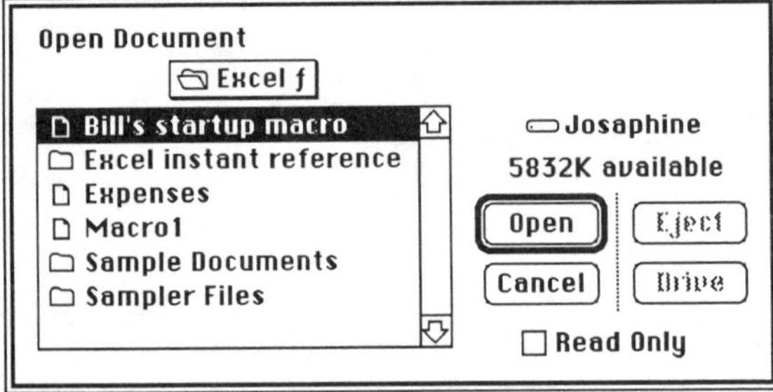

SYNTAX

OPEN(<*document_name*>**,**
<*update_or_not*>**,**<*read_only*>**)**
OPEN?()

EQUIVALENT COMMAND

File Open

USAGE

The OPEN() macro function is used to open existing documents. Enter the name of the document to open as a string. If the document is not in the current directory, Excel will put up a dialog box asking you to find it. To access files on other drives or directories, either include the directory path with the document name or change the current directory with the DIRECTORY() macro function. See the Introduction for the syntax of a path.

<update_or_not> is a numeric code to update any external references to unopened documents. The allowed values are 0 (do not update) and 1 (update external references). This is ignored if there are no external references. If it is omitted, a dialog box will pop up asking you whether you want to update. (FALSE and TRUE may be used for codes 0 and 1, respectively.)

The *<read_only>* argument is in version 1.03 or later. It causes the document to open as read-only if it is TRUE, or normally if it is FALSE or omitted.

The OPEN?() macro function takes no argument but shows the File Open dialog box instead.

SEE ALSO

CLOSE(), DIRECTORY(), OPEN.LINKS()

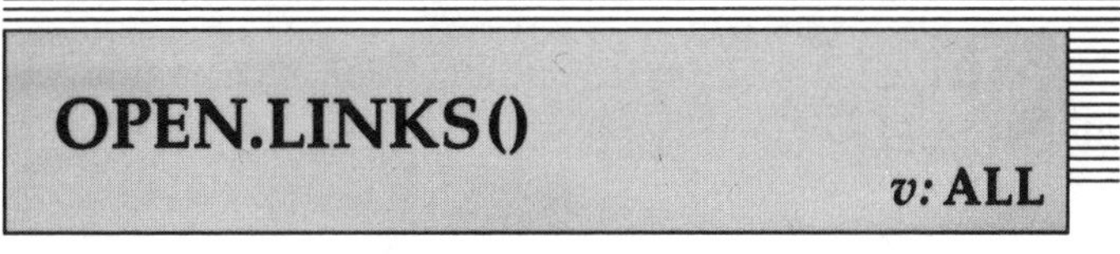

DIALOG BOX

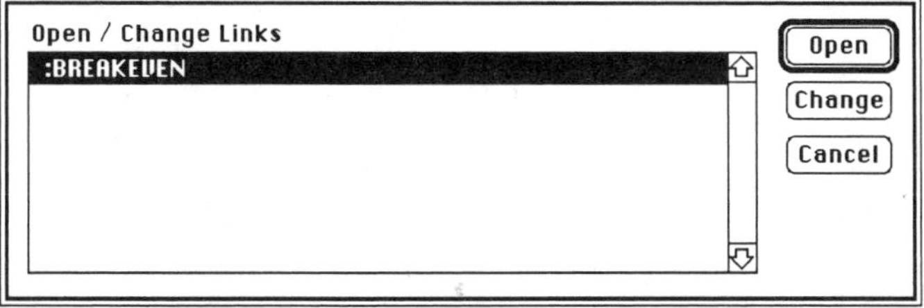

SYNTAX

OPEN.LINKS(<*document_list*>**)**
OPEN.LINKS?()

EQUIVALENT COMMAND

File Links

USAGE

The OPEN.LINKS() macro function, when combined with the LINKS() macro function, opens all documents on which the active document is dependent. Alone, OPEN.LINKS() opens any list of files supplied in the argument.

The list of document names is an array of strings, with each string containing the name of a document to open. If the files are in the current directory, only their names are needed. To access files on other drives and directories, either include the directory path with the document name or change the current directory with the DIRECTORY() macro function. See the Introduction for the syntax of a path.

The OPEN.LINKS?() macro function takes no argument, but shows the File Links dialog box instead.

SEE ALSO

CHANGE.LINK(), CLOSE(), DIRECTORY(), LINKS(), OPEN()

OVERLAY.CHART.TYPE()

v: ALL

DIALOG BOX

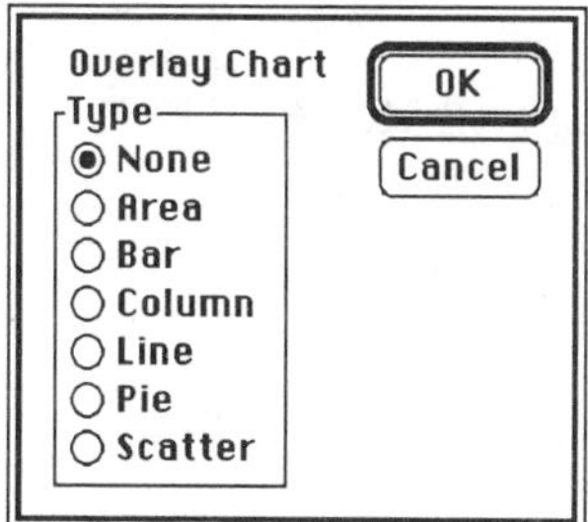

SYNTAX

OVERLAY.CHART.TYPE(*<chart_type>*)
OVERLAY.CHART.TYPE?()

EQUIVALENT COMMAND

Chart Overlay Chart Type

USAGE

The OVERLAY.CHART.TYPE() macro function is used to set the type of the overlay chart. The allowed values are 1 (none), 2 (area chart), 3 (bar chart), 4 (column chart), 5 (line chart), 6 (pie chart), and 7 (scatter chart). Note that these codes differ by 1 from those used with the MAIN.CHART.TYPE() macro function. Excel allows you to split the plotting of your data series between two different chart types. The first, or default, is the main chart. The second is the overlay chart. Set the main chart type with the MAIN.CHART.TYPE() macro function. Assign data series to the main chart and overlay chart with the Format Main Chart and Format Overlay Chart commands.

The OVERLAY.CHART.TYPE?() macro function takes no argument, but shows the Chart Overlay Chart Type dialog box instead.

SEE ALSO

GALLERY.xxxx(), MAIN.CHART.TYPE()

PAGE.SETUP()

v: ALL

DIALOG BOX

For a TTY printer:

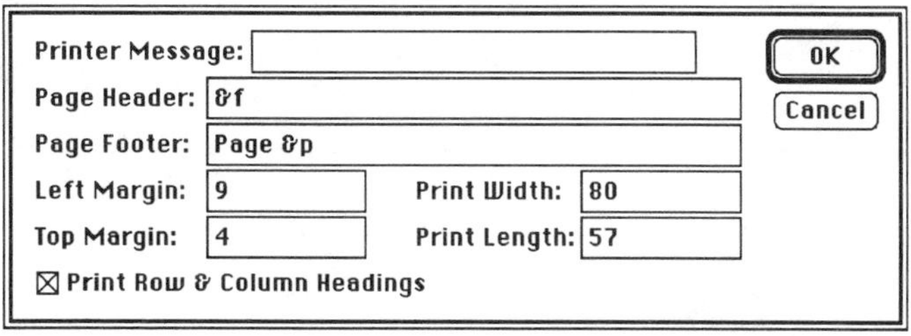

Printer Message: [ ] OK

Page Header: &f Cancel

Page Footer: Page &p

Left Margin: 9 Print Width: 80

Top Margin: 4 Print Length: 57

☒ Print Row & Column Headings

For a worksheet or macro set and a Macintosh Printer:

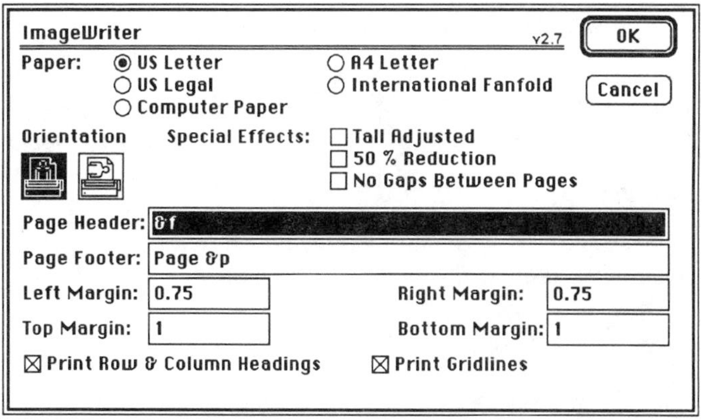

ImageWriter v2.7 OK

Paper: ◉ US Letter ○ A4 Letter

○ US Legal ○ International Fanfold Cancel

○ Computer Paper

Orientation Special Effects: ☐ Tall Adjusted

☐ 50 % Reduction

☐ No Gaps Between Pages

Page Header: &f

Page Footer: Page &p

Left Margin: 0.75 Right Margin: 0.75

Top Margin: 1 Bottom Margin: 1

☒ Print Row & Column Headings ☒ Print Gridlines

For a chart and a Macintosh printer:

ImageWriter v2.7 OK
Paper: ◉ US Letter ○ A4 Letter
○ US Legal ○ International Fanfold Cancel
○ Computer Paper
Orientation Special Effects: ☐ Tall Adjusted
☐ 50 % Reduction
☐ No Gaps Between Pages
Page Header: &f
Page Footer: Page &p
Left Margin: 0.75 Print Width: 7
Top Margin: 1 Print Height: 9
○ Screen Size ◉ Fit to Page

SYNTAX

For a TTY printer:

PAGE.SETUP(*<header_string>***,***<footer_string>***,**
*<left_margin>***,***<print_width>***,***<top_margin>***,**
*<print_length>***,***<headings_or_not>***,***<printer_setup_string>***)**

For a worksheet or macro sheet and a Macintosh printer:

PAGE.SETUP(*<header_string>***,***<footer_string>***,**
*<left_margin>***,***<right_margin>***,***<top_margin>***,**
*<bottom_margin>***,***<headings_or_not>***,***<gridlines_or_not>***)**

For a chart and a Macintosh printer:

PAGE.SETUP(*<header_string>***,***<footer_string>***,**
*<left_margin>***,***<print_width>***,***<top_margin>***,***<print_length>***,**
*<size>***)**

EQUIVALENT COMMAND

File Page Setup

USAGE

The PAGE.SETUP() macro function is used to set the size of the printed part of the page and to set headers and footers. There are three variations of the command, depending on the printer type and the window to be printed. The first version is for a worksheet or macro sheet printed on a TTY-type printer (that is, a character-only printer) set with the File Printer Setup command. The second is for printing a worksheet or macro sheet on a Macintosh Printer. The third is for printing a chart on a Macintosh printer.

The headers and footers are strings to print one-half inch below the top of the page and one half inch above the bottom of the page. The strings can be formatted with the following printer codes:

CODE	FUNCTION
&L	align left
&C	center
&R	align right
&P	insert page number
&D	insert date
&T	insert time
&F	insert document name
&B	print bold
&I	print italic
&&	insert an ampersand

The margins set the printed portion of the page. If the printer selected with the File Printer Setup is a Macintosh printer, these measurements are in inches; otherwise, they are in characters.

The two flags, *<headings_or_not>* and *<gridlines_or_not>*, set whether row and column headings, and gridlines, respectively, are printed. A value of TRUE prints the headings or gridlines; FALSE does not. If either is omitted, the previous value is assumed.

For a TTY-type printer, you can send a <*printer_setup_string*> to initialize the printer and set the character size. To send control characters, preface the character with a caret. For example, ^[sends the escape character.

The size code determines whether a chart is printed the same size shown on the screen or expanded to fit the printable area on the page. The allowed values are 1 (screen size) and 2 (fit to the page). If it is omitted, the previous value is assumed.

The PAGE.SETUP?() macro function takes no argument, but shows one of the File Page Setup dialog boxes instead. The top half of the two Macintosh printer dialog boxes contain the standard Macintosh printer options, which depend on the printer type.

SEE ALSO

PRINT(), PRINTER.SETUP()

PASTE()

v: **ALL**

SYNTAX

PASTE()

EQUIVALENT COMMAND

Edit Paste

USAGE

If the insertion point is in the formula bar, the PASTE() macro function inserts the contents of the clipboard there. If the insertion point is a cell on the worksheet or macro sheet, PASTE() inserts the contents of the active Cut or Copy selection at the insertion point. If a chart is the active document, PASTE() inserts the values in the active Cut or Copy selection as a new data series on the chart.

SEE ALSO

CANCEL.COPY(), COPY(), COPY.CHART(), COPY.PICTURE(), CUT(), PASTE.SPECIAL()

PASTE.SPECIAL()

v: **ALL**

DIALOG BOX

Worksheet to worksheet:

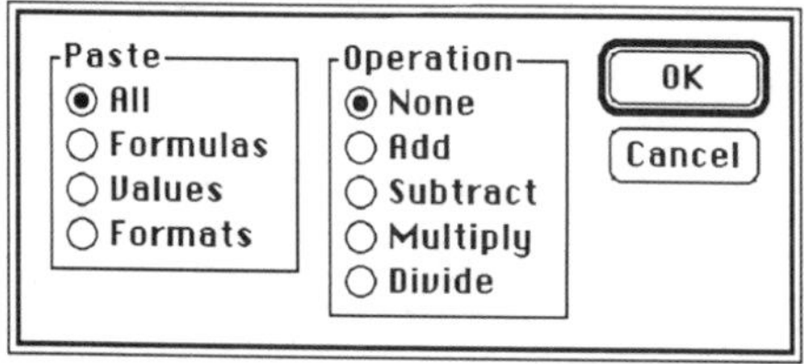

Worksheet to chart:

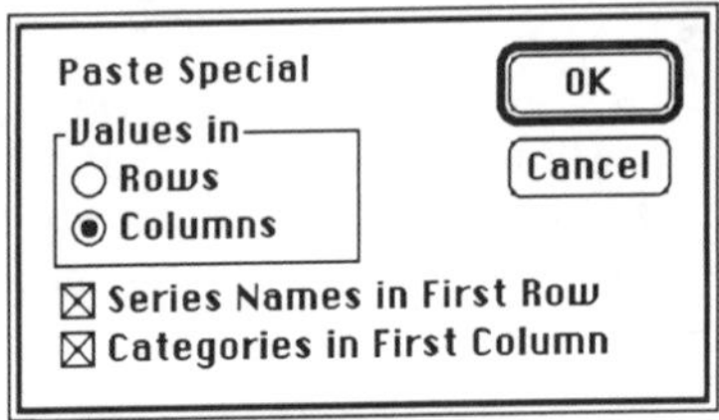

Chart to chart:

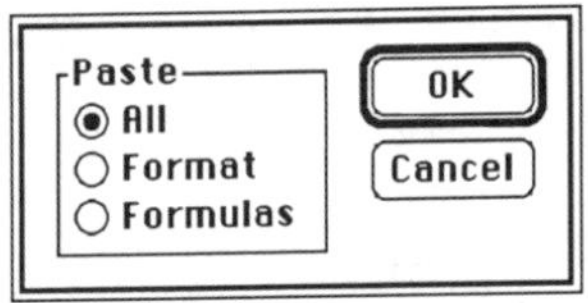

SYNTAX

Worksheet to worksheet:

PASTE.SPECIAL(<*cell_parts*>**,**<*operation*>**)**
PASTE.SPECIAL?()

Worksheet to chart:

PASTE.SPECIAL(<*rows_or_columns*>**,**
<*names_in_selection*>**,**<*categories_in_selection*>**)**
PASTE.SPECIAL?()

Chart to chart:

PASTE.SPECIAL(<*chart_parts*>**)**
PASTE.SPECIAL?()

EQUIVALENT COMMAND

Edit Paste Special

USAGE

The first version of the PASTE.SPECIAL() macro function is equivalent to the Edit Paste Special command when you are copying data from a worksheet or macro sheet range to another worksheet or macro sheet range. The *<cell_parts>* argument determines what component of the contents of the cells to paste into the active selection. The allowed values are 1 (all), 2 (formulas), 3 (values), and 4 (formats). The *<operation>* argument determines how the copied data will be inserted into the active selection. If *<operation>* is 1 (none), the copied data replaces any data in the active selection. If *<operation>* is 2 through 5, the copied data is combined with the data in the active selection according to the operation specified by the code: 2 (add), 3 (subtract), 4 (multiply), or 5 (divide).

The second version is equivalent to the Edit Paste Special command when you are copying data from a worksheet or macro sheet range to a chart. The *<rows_and_columns>* argument specifies whether separate data series in the copied selection are in separate rows (a value of 1) or columns (2). The *<names_in_selection>* argument specifies whether the first column or row contains the series names. A value of TRUE means the names are in the selection; FALSE means they are not. The *<categories_in_selection>* argument specifies whether the first row or column contains category data (a value of TRUE) or another data series of values (FALSE).

The third version is equivalent to the Edit Paste Special command when you are copying data from a chart to a chart. The *<chart_parts>* argument determines what parts of the chart to paste into the selected chart. The allowed values are 1 (all), 2 (formats), and 3 (formulas).

The PASTE.SPECIAL?() macro function takes no argument, but shows one of the Edit Paste Special dialog boxes instead.

SEE ALSO

CANCEL.COPY(), COPY(), COPY.CHART(), COPY.PICTURE(), CUT(), PASTE()

PRECISION()

v: **ALL**

SYNTAX

PRECISION(<*as_displayed_or_full*>)

EQUIVALENT COMMAND

Option Full Precision
Option Precision As Displayed

USAGE

The PRECISION() macro function sets the way data shown on the worksheet is stored. Full precision stores 14 decimal places, even if only 2 or 3 are showing. Precision as displayed truncates all numbers after the last displayed value. This is used in financial calculations to insure that fractions of a cent are always rounded to full cents.

The allowed argument values are TRUE (use full precision) and FALSE (use the displayed precision). If it is omitted, the value will alternate each time the command is executed.

PREFERRED()

v: ALL

SYNTAX

PREFERRED()

EQUIVALENT COMMAND

Gallery Preferred

USAGE

The PREFERRED() macro function sets the format of the current chart to the preferred format. The format of a chart consists of everything about the chart but the data series, arrows, and unattached strings; it includes the chart type, axis types and labels, format of the text, legend, and any colors that are on the chart. A column chart is the default at startup. The preferred format is set by creating a chart in the desired format and then executing the Chart Set Preferred Format command.

PRINT()

v: ALL

DIALOG BOX

TTY Printer:

Page Range: ◉ All ○ From: [ ] To: [ ] OK
Copies: 1 Cancel
Paper Feed: ◉ Continuous ○ Cut Sheet

Macintosh Printer:

ImageWriter v2.7 OK
Quality: ○ Best ◉ Faster ○ Draft
Page Range: ◉ All ○ From: [ ] To: [ ] Cancel
Copies: 1
Paper Feed: ◉ Automatic ○ Hand Feed
☐ Page Preview ☐ Print Using Color

SYNTAX

PRINT(<*range*>,<*from*>,<*to*>,<*copies*>,<*draft*>,
<*preview*>,<*parts*>,<*color*>,<*feed*>**)**
PRINT()
PRINT?()

EQUIVALENT COMMAND

File Print

USAGE

Use commas as place holders for the arguments that do not apply in your situation. If the printer type is TTY, set with the File Printer Setup command, only the arguments *<range>*, *<from>*, *<to>*, *<copies>*, and *<feed>* will have any effect. Enter *<range>*, the pages of the document to print, as a numeric code. The allowed values are 1 (all) and 2 (from/to). Input the pages to print from and to in the next two arguments.

Enter *<from>*, the starting page of a print range, as an integer. It is needed only if *<range>* is 2.

Enter *<to>*, the ending page of a print range, as an integer. It is needed only if *<range>* is 2.

Enter the number of *<copies>* to print as an integer.

<preview> (Version 1.5) is a flag to preview the printed pages on the screen, as a logical value. The allowed values are TRUE (preview the pages) and FALSE (print the pages).

<color> (Version 1.5) is a flag to print in color or not, entered as a logical value. The allowed values are TRUE (print in color) and FALSE (print in black and white).

<feed> indicates the type of sheet feeder to use on the printer, entered as a numeric code. The allowed values are 1 (continuous forms) and 2 (single sheets).

The second form of the function retains all of the settings of the previous call to the PRINT() command, except that *<range>* is reset to all, *<copies>* is reset to 1, and *<feed>* is reset to continuous.

The PRINT?() macro function takes no argument, but shows one of the File Print dialog boxes instead.

The *<draft>* and *<parts>* arguments are in version 1.5 or later, but have no effect on the Macintosh. They are included for compatibility with Excel for the PC.

SEE ALSO

PAGE.SETUP(), PRINTER.SETUP(), SET.PRINT.AREA()

PRINTER.SETUP()

v: **ALL**

DIALOG BOX

Printer Setup
Macintosh
TTY
Port
Printer
Modem
Baud
300
600
1200
2400
4800
9600
OK
Cancel

SYNTAX

PRINTER.SETUP(*<printer>*[,*<printer_port>*,*<baud_rate>*])
PRINTER.SETUP?()

EQUIVALENT COMMAND

File Printer Setup

USAGE

The PRINTER.SETUP() macro function is used to set the type of printer and the printer port and speed.

Enter your printer type as a numeric code. The allowed values are 1 (Macintosh) and 2 (TTY).

If the printer is type 2 (TTY), enter the printer port and baud rate as numeric codes. The allowed values of *<printer_port>* are 1 (printer) and 2 (modem), and the allowed values of

<baud_rate> are 1 (300), 2 (600), 3 (1200), 4 (2400), 5 (4800), and 6 (9600).

The PRINTER.SETUP?() macro function takes no argument, but shows the File Printer Setup dialog box instead.

SEE ALSO

PAGE.SETUP(), PRINT()

PROTECT.DOCUMENT()

***v:* ALL**

SYNTAX

PROTECT.DOCUMENT([*<protect_contents>*]**)**
PROTECT.DOCUMENT?()

EQUIVALENT COMMAND

Options Protect Document
Options Unprotect Document

USAGE

The PROTECT.DOCUMENT() macro function is used to turn on cell protection. Protected cells can be locked, hidden, or both. The type of protection is set with the CELL.PROTECTION() macro function but not activated until the document is protected with the PROTECT.DOCUMENT() macro function.

<protect_contents> is a flag to protect or unprotect the contents of the active document. The allowed values are TRUE (protect the contents) and FALSE (unprotect the contents). If it is omitted, the value will alternate.

To use a password with the cell protection, use the PROTECT.DOCUMENT?() form of the function. It will then request a password with a dialog box.

SEE ALSO

CELL.PROTECTION(), UNLOCKED.NEXT(), UNLOCKED.PREV()

QUIT()

v: **1.5**

SYNTAX

QUIT()

EQUIVALENT COMMAND

File Quit

USAGE

When the QUIT() macro function is executed, Excel closes all documents, checks for any unsaved documents, inquires if you want to save any unsaved documents, saves the ones you indicate, and then quits.

REFTEXT()

v: **1.5**

SYNTAX

REFTEXT(<*reference*>,<*reference_style*>)

EQUIVALENT COMMAND

None

USAGE

The REFTEXT() macro function converts a reference into a text string as an absolute reference. The style of the reference in the string is determined by the second argument. The allowed values are TRUE (use the A1 style) and FALSE (use the R1C1 style). If it is omitted, it is assumed to be FALSE. When a reference is the result of a formula, it is generally not possible to see it, because it is usually converted immediately into the value of that reference. Use REFTEXT() to see the reference generated rather than its value. It is also useful to convert a reference to text, so that it can be edited and then converted back to a reference with TEXTREF().

SEE ALSO

TEXTREF()

RELREF()

v: **ALL**

SYNTAX

RELREF(<*reference_1*>,<*reference_2*>**)**

EQUIVALENT COMMAND

None

USAGE

The RELREF() macro function returns a string containing <*reference_1*> as a relative reference, in the R1C1 style, relative to the upper-left corner of <*reference_2*>.

SEE ALSO

ABSREF(), OFFSET()

REMOVE.PAGE.BREAK()

v: **ALL**

SYNTAX

REMOVE.PAGE.BREAK()

EQUIVALENT COMMAND

Options Remove Page Break

USAGE

The REMOVE.PAGE.BREAK() macro function is used to remove any page breaks inserted with the Options Set Page Break command or the SET.PAGE.BREAK() macro function. If a manually inserted page break is above or to the left of the active cell, it will be removed.

SEE ALSO

SET.PAGE.BREAK()

RENAME.COMMAND()

v: **1.5**

SYNTAX

RENAME.COMMAND(*<bar_number>***,***<menu_position>***,** *<command_position>***,***<new_name>***)**

EQUIVALENT COMMAND

None

USAGE

The RENAME.COMMAND() macro function changes the name of a custom command. Only custom commands created with the ADD.MENU() and ADD.COMMAND() macro functions can be changed. Attempting to change the name of the built-in commands on the built-in menu bars (see the ADD.BAR() macro function) will cause a macro error.

Enter the menu *<bar number>* as a numeric code. The allowed values are 1 through 21. Values 1 through 3 are for Excel's built-in menu bars. Values 4 through 6 are reserved for future versions. Values 7 through 21 are for custom menu bars. See the ADD.BAR() macro function for more information.

Enter *<menu_position>*, the menu on the menu bar as either a string containing the menu name or the number of its position. Position numbers count from the left with the first menu as number 1. (The Apple menu is not counted.)

Enter *<command_position>*, the command on the menu to rename, as either a string containing the command name or the number of its position. Position numbers count from the top with the first command as number 1. Horizontal bars used for command separators are also counted.

Enter the <*new_name*> for the command as a string.

SEE ALSO

ADD.BAR(), ADD.COMMAND(), ADD.MENU(), CHECK.COMMAND(), DELETE.BAR(), DELETE.COMMAND(), DELETE.MENU(), ENABLE.COMMAND(), GET.BAR(), RENAME.COMMAND(), SHOW.BAR()

RESULT()

v: **ALL**

SYNTAX

RESULT(<*result_type*>**)**

EQUIVALENT COMMAND

None

USAGE

The RESULT() macro function sets the type of value returned by a function macro when the RETURN() function is executed. The allowed <*result_type*> values are 1 (number), 2 (string), 4 (logical), 8 (reference), 16 (error), 64 (array), or any combination of these codes added together. RESULT() is optional for all types except for an array or reference, where it is required. Excel will check the value being returned, and attempt to convert it to the required type if it is not correct. If it cannot convert it, it will return the error value #VALUE!.

SEE ALSO

ARGUMENT(), RETURN()

RETURN()

v: **ALL**

SYNTAX

RETURN([<*value*>])

EQUIVALENT COMMAND

None

USAGE

The RETURN() macro function ends the execution of a macro and returns to the calling function. If the macro was called with the Macro Run command, control is returned to the user. If it was called by another macro, control is returned to the next executable statement, along with the value of the function. If it was called from within a formula, the value is returned and the formula continues calculating. The type of value returned can be set with the RESULT() macro function.

SEE ALSO

SUBROUTINES, RESULT()

RUN()

v: **ALL**

DIALOG BOX

SYNTAX

RUN(<*macro_reference*>**)**
RUN?()

EQUIVALENT COMMAND

Macro Run

USAGE

The argument to the RUN() macro function can be an external cell reference, a string with the macro name as shown in the Macro Run dialog box, or a string containing a cell reference in the R1C1 style. Any values returned by the macro will be returned by the RUN() macro function. You may not pass arguments to the macro with the RUN() macro function, as you can when you call the function by reference (see **SUBROUTINES**).

The RUN?() macro function takes no argument, but shows the Macro Run dialog box instead.

SEE ALSO

GOTO(), SUBROUTINES

SAVE()

v: **ALL**

SYNTAX

SAVE()

EQUIVALENT COMMAND

File Save

USAGE

The SAVE() macro function saves the active document to disk. If the document has not been saved before, it will be saved in the current directory, with its current name. You will not be prompted for a new name and directory as with the File Save command. Use the SAVE.AS() macro function to change the file name, type or directory, even for new documents.

SEE ALSO

CLOSE(), OPEN(), SAVE.AS()

SAVE.AS()

v: ALL

DIALOG BOX

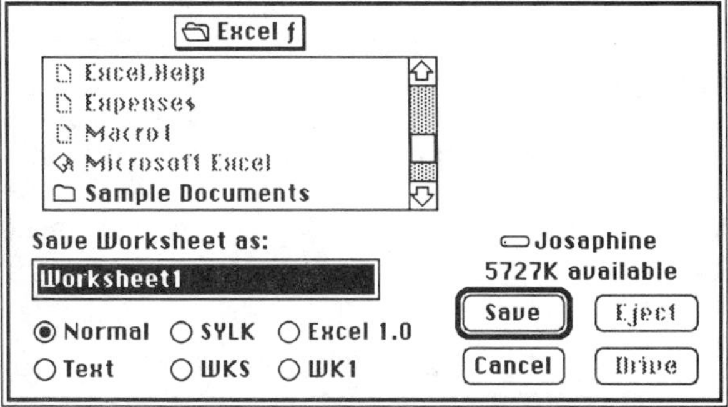

SYNTAX

SAVE.AS(<*name_string*>,<*file_type*>**)**
SAVE.AS?()

EQUIVALENT COMMAND

File Save

USAGE

The SAVE.AS() macro function saves the active document to disk in the current directory, with its name specified as <*name_string*> and with a file type of <*file_type*>. The allowed values of <*file_type*> are 1 (Normal), 2 (SYLK), 3 (text),

4 (WKS), 5 (WK1), and 10 (Excel 1.0). To save it in a different directory, use the DIRECTORY() macro function to change the current directory, include the directory path with the file name, or use the SAVE.AS?() form of the function. See the Introduction for the syntax of a directory path. Use this function to set the name of a new document, or to set the file type to something other than normal. Use it also to change the name of a document or file type.

The normal file type is the standard format for the version of Excel that you are using. The SYLK file type is Microsoft's file interchange format. It is a text format that is readable by most Microsoft products. It is also useful for transferring files between the Macintosh and the PC. The file types WKS and WK1 are for Lotus 1-2-3 Versions 1 and 2 respectively. The Excel 1.0 format is for saving a file to be used with the earlier version of Excel.

The SAVE.AS?() macro function takes no argument, but shows the File Save As dialog box instead.

SEE ALSO

CLOSE(), OPEN(), SAVE()

SELECT()

v: **ALL**

SYNTAX

SELECT([<*selection*>**][,**<*active_cell*>**])**

EQUIVALENT COMMAND

None, but see below

USAGE

The SELECT() macro function is equivalent to selecting cells on the worksheet or macro sheet. It is similar in function to the FORMULA.GOTO() macro function. Use it to select a cell or a range of cells and scroll the worksheet or macro sheet until they are in view. If *<selection>* is a relative reference in the R1C1 style, it is assumed to be relative to the current active cell. If it is omitted, the current cell selection is not changed. Use the *<active_cell>* argument to move the active cell within the selection range. If *<selection>* is omitted, *<active_cell>* must be inside the current selection. If *<active_cell>* is omitted, the upper-left corner of *<selection>* is used.

SEE ALSO

ACTIVE.CELL() FORMULA.GOTO(), SELECTION()

SELECT.CHART()

v: **ALL**

SYNTAX

SELECT.CHART()

EQUIVALENT COMMAND

Chart Select Chart

USAGE

The SELECT.CHART() macro function is equivalent to the Chart Select Chart command. When executed, the whole chart is selected. Once selected, a chart can be copied and cleared, the text format changed, and the background and border set.

Copying a selected chart with the COPY() macro function will copy almost everything on the chart. If you paste it to another chart, everything will appear but the unattached text and the arrows. Use the PASTE.SPECIAL() macro function to control what parts are pasted.

Changing the text format of a selected chart will change it everywhere on the chart. Patterns and borders will apply only to the rectangle that surrounds the whole chart. To put a border and a background area around only the plot area, use the Chart Select Plot Area command.

SEE ALSO

COPY(), **Format Patterns...** command,
Format Text... command

SELECT.LAST.CELL()

***v:* ALL**

SYNTAX

SELECT.LAST.CELL()

EQUIVALENT COMMAND

Formula Select Last Cell

USAGE

The SELECT.LAST.CELL() macro function selects the cell at the intersection of the last row and last column that contains a value, formula, or even a format. Excel uses memory for every cell in the rectangle that has cell A1 as the upper-left corner and the last cell as the lower-right corner. Even formatting a cell outside of your work area on a worksheet can increase memory use. To minimize the use of memory, try to keep the part of the worksheet that you use in as compact a rectangle as possible.

SEE ALSO

GOTO(), SELECT()

SELECTION()

v: **ALL**

SYNTAX

SELECTION()

EQUIVALENT COMMAND

None

USAGE

The SELECTION() macro function returns the reference of the current selection as an external reference. Contrast this to the ACTIVE.CELL() macro function, which returns only the active cell in the current selection.

The REFTEXT() macro function can be used to change the reference into text so that you can read it. Otherwise, all you will see is the contents of the reference, rather than the reference itself.

SEE ALSO

ACTIVE.CELL(), SELECT()

SET.CRITERIA()

v: **ALL**

SYNTAX

SET.CRITERIA()

EQUIVALENT COMMAND

Data Set Criteria

USAGE

The SET.CRITERIA() macro function defines the criteria range for searching a database and the name *Criteria* as the currently selected cells. A criteria range consists of one row of cells containing the field names from the database, and at least one row containing selection criteria. There can be more than one row of selection criteria, with each row a logical OR in relation to the other rows. See the Introduction for more information about databases.

SEE ALSO

DATA.DELETE(), DATA.FIND(), DATA.FIND.NEXT(), DATA.FIND.PREV(), EXTRACT(), SET.DATABASE()

SET.DATABASE()

v: **ALL**

SYNTAX

SET.DATABASE()

EQUIVALENT COMMAND

Data Set Database

USAGE

The SET.DATABASE() macro function defines the database range and the name *Database* as the currently selected cells. The first row of cells in the database range contains the field names for the records in the database. The following rows contain the records of the database, one record per row. See the Introduction for more information about databases.

SEE ALSO

DATA.DELETE(), DATA.FIND(), DATA.FIND.NEXT(), DATA.FIND.PREV(), EXTRACT(), SET.CRITERIA()

SET.NAME()

v: **ALL**

SYNTAX

SET.NAME(<*name_string*>,<*definition*>**)**

EQUIVALENT COMMAND

None

USAGE

The SET.NAME() macro function creates and defines a name on the currently executing macro sheet. If the name already exists, it will be redefined. The definition can be a number, string, logical value, formula, or reference. If the definition is a formula, the formula will be evaluated first, and the result will be used for the definition. If the definition is a reference, it will be the reference itself, not the contents of the reference. Use the DEREF() macro function if you want the definition to be the contents of the reference.

Note that the value of a defined name is not stored in a cell, and thus does not take up any of the cells on the macro sheet.

Use the SET.VALUE() macro function to change the value of cells on the macro sheet, and the FORMULA() macro function to change the value of cells on a worksheet.

To see a list of the current definitions, execute the Formula Define Name command and select the definition you are interested in. Quit the command with Cancel, so you do not change any of your definitions. You can get the name that goes with a definition with the GET.DEF() macro function, or get the definition that goes with a name with the GET.NAME() macro function.

SEE ALSO

CREATE.NAMES(), DEFINE.NAME(), DELETE.NAME(), GET.DEF(), GET.NAME(), SET.VALUE()

SET.PAGE.BREAK()

v: **ALL**

SYNTAX

SET.PAGE.BREAK()

EQUIVALENT COMMAND

Options Set Page Break

USAGE

The SET.PAGE.BREAK() macro function is used to insert page breaks manually above and to the left of the active cell.

SEE ALSO

REMOVE.PAGE.BREAK()

SET.PRINT.AREA()

v: **ALL**

SYNTAX

SET.PRINT.AREA()

EQUIVALENT COMMAND

Options Set Print Area

USAGE

The SET.PRINT.AREA() macro function defines the name *Print_Area* as the current selection. When the print command is executed, only the area defined by *Print_Area* will be printed. If *Print_Area* is not defined, the whole worksheet is selected.

To delete the print area, execute the macro command DELETE.NAME("!Print_Area").

To see the current print area, execute the command Formula Define Name and select *Print_Area* if it exists. The definition will appear in the "Refers to:" box. You can also select the print area by executing the Formula Goto command and selecting *Print_Area*. To get the print area of the active sheet, use the GET.NAME() macro function with "!Print_Area" as the argument.

SEE ALSO

FORMULA.GOTO(), GET.NAME(), PRINT(), SET.PRINT.TITLES()

SET.PRINT.TITLES()

v: **ALL**

SYNTAX

SET.PRINT.TITLES()

EQUIVALENT COMMAND

Options Set Print Titles

USAGE

The SET.PRINT.TITLES() macro function defines the name *Print_Titles* as the currently selected row and/or column. When the sheet is printed, the contents of this row and/or column, in the same rows and/or columns as the printed cells, is printed adjacent to the row and column headings. The selection can consist of a row, several adjacent rows, a column, several adjacent columns, or a combination of adjacent rows and adjacent columns. Select a row and a column at the same time by holding down the Command key. The print titles do not have to be in the current print area defined with the Options Print Area command.

To delete the print titles, execute the macro function DELETE.NAME("!Print_Titles").

To see the current print titles, execute the Formula Define Name command and select *Print_Titles* if it exists. The definition will appear in the Refers To box. You can also execute the Formula Goto command and select *Print_Titles* to select the print titles area. In a macro, use the GET.NAME() macro function with "!Print_Titles" as the argument, to get the print titles of the active sheet.

SEE ALSO

FORMULA.GOTO(), GET.NAME(), PRINT(), PRINT.AREA()

SET.VALUE()

***v:* ALL**

SYNTAX

SET.VALUE(<*reference*>,<*value*>**)**

EQUIVALENT COMMAND

None

USAGE

The SET.VALUE() macro function sets the value of cells on the currently executing macro sheet. (<*value*>) can be a number, string, logical value, formula, or reference. If it is a formula or reference, it will be evaluated first, before its value is assigned to the reference. Note that if the reference contains a macro function or formula, it will not be changed by this command; only the cell's value is changed.

Use the SET.NAME() macro function to create or change name definitions on the macro sheet, and the FORMULA() macro function to change the value of cells on a worksheet.

SEE ALSO

FORMULA(), SET.VALUE()

SHOW.ACTIVE.CELL()

v: **ALL**

SYNTAX

SHOW.ACTIVE.CELL()

EQUIVALENT COMMAND

Formula Show Active Cell

USAGE

The SHOW.ACTIVE.CELL() macro function causes the current sheet to scroll until the active cell is visible. It is useful for finding the active cell after you have scrolled away from it.

SEE ALSO

FORMULA.FIND(), FORMULA.GOTO()

SHOW.BAR()

v: **1.5**

SYNTAX

SHOW.BAR([<*bar_number*>]**)**

EQUIVALENT COMMAND

None

USAGE

The SHOW.BAR() macro function displays a new menu bar. The bar can be one of the built-in menu bars (see the ADD.BAR() macro function) or a custom menu bar created with the ADD.BAR() macro function. If any one of the built-in menu bars is selected, only the one that is appropriate for the active window will be displayed.

The menu <*bar_number*> is entered as a numeric code. The allowed values are 1 through 21. Values 1 through 3 are for Excel's built-in menu bars (see the **ADD.BAR()** macro function). Values 4 through 6 are reserved for later versions. Values 7 through 21 are for custom menu bars defined with the ADD.BAR() macro function. If the code is omitted, the appropriate built-in bar will be displayed.

SEE ALSO

ADD.BAR(), ADD.COMMAND(), ADD.MENU(), CHECK.COMMAND(), DELETE.BAR(), DELETE.COMMAND(), DELETE.MENU(), ENABLE.COMMAND(), GET.BAR(), RENAME.COMMAND()

SHOW.CLIPBOARD() *v:* ALL

SYNTAX

SHOW.CLIPBOARD()

EQUIVALENT COMMAND

Window Show Clipboard

USAGE

The SHOW.CLIPBOARD() macro function opens the clipboard window, displaying the contents of the clipboard.

SIZE() *v:* ALL

SYNTAX

SIZE(<*width*>,<*height*>[,<*window_name*>]**)**

EQUIVALENT COMMAND

None, but see below

USAGE

The SIZE() macro function is equivalent to dragging the size box on the window. The upper-left corner is held fixed, and the lower-right corner is moved until the window is the new size. A window can be resized without activating it.

The desired *<width>* and *<height>* of the window are entered, as integers, in points. A point is 1/72 inch. The name of the window to resize, *<window_name>*, is entered as a string. If it is omitted, the active window is assumed.

SEE ALSO

FULL(), MOVE()

SORT()

***v:* ALL**

DIALOG BOX

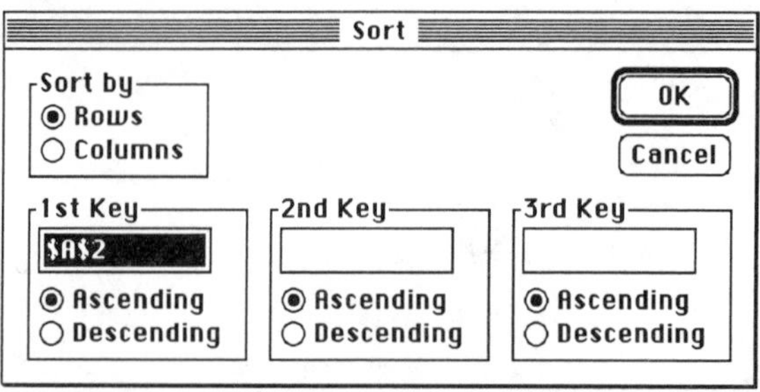

SYNTAX

SORT(*<sort_by>*,*<first_key>*,[*<sort_order>*]
[,*<second_key>*,[*<sort_order>*][,*<third_key>*,
[*<sort_order>*]]]**)**
SORT?()

EQUIVALENT COMMAND

Data Sort

USAGE

The SORT() macro function is used to sort the current selection. The *<sort_by>* argument indicates whether to sort by rows (1) or columns (2) using up to three columns or rows as the sort keys. The resulting selection will be sorted by the first key, and then the second, and finally the third. Each sort key is entered as a cell reference to the column (if sorting by rows) or the row (if sorting by columns), or a string containing a reference in the R1C1 style. If you use relative references in strings for the sort keys, they will be relative to the upper-left cell of the selection. *<sort_order>* is entered as a numeric code. The allowed values are 1 (ascending) and 2 (descending). If it is omitted, ascending is assumed.

The SORT?() macro function takes no argument, but shows the Data Sort dialog box instead.

SPLIT()

v: 1.5

SYNTAX

SPLIT([<*column_split*>][,<*row_split*>])

EQUIVALENT COMMAND

None, but see below

USAGE

The SPLIT() macro function is equivalent to dragging the split bars in a window to split that window into two or four panes. Each pane can then be scrolled separately with its own scroll bars. The arguments refer to the row and column in the current window and not to the row or column of the sheet. <*column_split*> is the column number in the current window to split to the right of. If it is 0, any previous split is removed. If it is omitted, any previous split is unchanged. <*row_split*> is the current row to split below. If it is 0, any previous split is removed. If it is omitted, any previous split is unchanged.

The FREEZE.PANES() macro function can be used to lock the upper and/or left panes of the window, so that they cannot be scrolled. This is usually done to keep titles in view, no matter where you scroll in the sheet.

SEE ALSO

FREEZE.PANES()

STEP()

v: ALL

DIALOG BOX

Single Step

Cell: Macro1!A2

Formula:
=RETURN()

Step

Halt

Continue

SYNTAX

STEP()

EQUIVALENT COMMAND

None

USAGE

The STEP() macro function causes a macro to pause between each command and put up the dialog box shown here, which allows you to step, halt, or continue. This function is used to debug macros.

SEE ALSO

HALT()

STYLE()

v: **ALL**

DIALOG BOX

Style
Bold
Italic
OK
Cancel

SYNTAX

STYLE(*<bold>*,*<italic>*)
STYLE?()

EQUIVALENT COMMAND

Format Style

USAGE

The STYLE() macro function sets the text style for strings in a cell. The two arguments correspond to the two check boxes in the dialog box. *<bold>* and *<italic>* are flags to set the style of the selected cells to bold and/or italic. The allowed values are TRUE (use the style) or FALSE (don't use the style).

The STYLE?() macro function takes no argument, but shows the Format Style dialog box instead.

SEE ALSO

ALIGNMENT(), CELL("prefix",<*reference*>**)** worksheet function, **BORDER(), CELL.PROTECTION(), FORMAT.NUMBER()**

SUBROUTINES

v: **ALL**

SYNTAX

<reference>(*<arguments>*)

EQUIVALENT COMMAND

None

USAGE

Use this syntax to call a macro from within a macro. When the called macro completes execution and hits a RETURN() macro function, the original macro will resume execution at the statement immediately after the <*reference*>() statement. This is in contrast to the GOTO() macro function, which is a one-way branch to another routine that cannot be returned from. Up to 13 arguments can be passed to the called macro (see the ARGUMENT() macro function) in the argument list; none, a single value, or an array of values can be returned to the calling macro. Because <*reference*> can be an external reference, a macro can call another macro on another open macro sheet. This is also the format to use to call a function macro from within a worksheet cell. As long as you include the name of the macro sheet that contains the macro you are calling, <*reference*> can be a simple cell reference to that sheet rather than a defined cell name, but the worksheet will be more readable if you do name the cell.

To run a macro with its name or reference in a string, use the RUN() macro function.

SEE ALSO

ARGUMENT(), GOTO(), RESULT(), RETURN(), RUN()

TABLE()

v: **ALL**

DIALOG BOX

Table

Row Input Cell:

Column Input Cell:

OK

Cancel

SYNTAX

TABLE([<*row_input_cell*>][,<*column_input_cell*>]**)**
TABLE?()

EQUIVALENT COMMAND

Data Table

USAGE

Use the TABLE() macro function to create a table of values from one or more formulas. Each argument is a cell reference or a string version of a cell reference in the R1C1 style. There are two types of tables, one-input and two-input. A one-input table inserts a row or column of numbers into a formula, to produce a row or column of values. Use only one of the two arguments for a one-input table. For a two-input table, use both arguments.

To create a one-input table, start with a rectangular region on a worksheet. The following paragraphs describe a table for columns of data; to create one in rows, just transpose these instructions.

Put the input data values in the first column, starting in the second row of the table. Put the formula to apply to these values in the first row, in the column that will contain the results. Have the formula refer to a cell outside this rectangular region. This is the input cell. Insert a reference to it as the <*column_input_cell*>. Select the rectangular region, including the input data and the formulas, but not including the input cell, and execute the Table command or function. All of the data in the first column will be inserted into the formula, and the result will be placed in the row of the cell containing the input data and the column of the cell containing the formula. In a one-input table, you can apply more than one formula to a single column of data. Place the other formulas to the right of the first formula, and reference the same input cell.

For a two-input table, place the formula in the upper-left corner of the rectangle and the two sets of input data in the first row and column. Place the two input cells somewhere outside the rectangle. Use references to these cells as the arguments to the function or command. Select the rectangle of cells, including the formula, and the row and column of input data. When the command is executed, Excel will create a two-dimensional table by applying the formula in the upper-left corner to the data in the top row and left column, and putting the value in the cell at the intersection of the row and column containing the input data.

Note that the formulas in the table can be simple references to the value of a formula, outside the table, that refers to the input cell.

The TABLE?() macro function takes no argument, but shows the Data Table dialog box instead.

TEXTREF()

***v:* 1.5**

SYNTAX

TEXTREF(<*reference_string*>[,<*A1_or_R1C1*>]**)**

EQUIVALENT COMMAND

None

USAGE

The TEXTREF() macro function converts a string representation of a reference into a reference. The reference can be in either A1 or R1C1 style; the style you use must be indicated as a logical value in the second argument. The allowed values are TRUE (A1 style) and FALSE (R1C1 style). If it is omitted, FALSE is assumed. This function is useful for changing a reference created by manipulating strings of text into a real reference. The inverse function, REFTEXT(), converts a reference into a string.

While TEXTREF() can convert external references, it cannot convert an unspecified external reference to the active sheet, such as "!A5".

SEE ALSO

REFTEXT()

UNDO()

v: ALL

SYNTAX

UNDO()

EQUIVALENT COMMAND

Edit Redo, Edit Undo

USAGE

The UNDO() macro function reverses the effect of the last action. Executing UNDO() a second time reverses the action of the first UNDO() function, redoing the changes. Note that most, but not all, actions can be undone.

UNLOCKED.NEXT/PREV()

v: 1.5

SYNTAX

UNLOCKED.NEXT()
UNLOCKED.PREV()

EQUIVALENT COMMAND

None, but see below

USAGE

The UNLOCKED.NEXT() and UNLOCKED.PREV() macro functions are equivalent to pressing Enter or Shift-Enter in a worksheet locked with the PROTECT.DOCUMENT() macro function or the Options Protect Document command. The active cell will move to the next or previous unlocked cell.

SEE ALSO

CELL.PROTECTION(), PROTECT.DOCUMENT()

VLINE/VPAGE/VSCROLL()

v: **ALL**

SYNTAX

VLINE(<*lines*>**)**
VPAGE(<*pages*>**)**
VSCROLL(<*row_number*>[,<*scroll_how*>]**)**

EQUIVALENT COMMAND

None

USAGE

The VLINE() macro function causes the active pane in the active window to be scrolled vertically by the number of lines specified in the argument.

The VPAGE() macro function causes the active pane of the active window to be scrolled vertically by the number of pages specified in the argument.

The VSCROLL() macro function scrolls the active pane of the active window to a specific row if <*scroll_how*> is TRUE, or to a row that is a certain fraction of the way down the sheet if <*scroll_how*> is FALSE, where a value of 0 is row 1 and 1 is row 16,384. Worksheets and macro sheets are 16,384 rows tall. <*scroll_how*> is in Versions 1.5 or later, and if it is omitted, FALSE is assumed.

SEE ALSO

HLINE/HPAGE/HSCROLL()

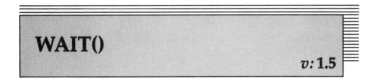

SYNTAX

WAIT(<*serial_day_number*>**)**

EQUIVALENT COMMAND

None

USAGE

The WAIT() macro function halts macro execution until <*serial_day_number*> is reached. A *serial day number* is a date expressed in days after January 1, 1904, and a time expressed in fractional parts of a day. Use this function to cause a macro to wait until a specific time before activating, or to pause for some amount of time. For example, to pause for five minutes, use the expression **=WAIT (NOW() + TIME (0,5,0))**.

WHILE()

v: **1.5**

SYNTAX

WHILE(<*logical_test*>**)**

EQUIVALENT COMMAND

None

USAGE

The WHILE() macro function starts the execution of WHILE()/NEXT() loop. The statements between the WHILE() statement and the NEXT() statement will be continuously executed until the value of *<logical_test>* is FALSE. If the argument is FALSE the first time WHILE() is encountered, the loop will be skipped.

SEE ALSO

BREAK(), FOR(), NEXT()

WINDOWS()

v: **ALL**

SYNTAX

WINDOWS()

EQUIVALENT COMMAND

None

USAGE

The WINDOWS() macro function returns a horizontal array of all currently open windows, ordered according to their level on the desktop. The first one is the active window, the second is the window just below the active window, and so on. Use the INDEX() function to select one name out of the array or enter it into a horizontal array of cells while holding down the Control key.

SEE ALSO

DIRECTORY(), DOCUMENTS(), LINKS()

Part 2:

Operators and Worksheet Functions

Operators

The operators in Excel are the basic building blocks for all mathematical calculations. They determine how values are combined to produce numeric results, logical comparisons, and strings. Table 2.1 lists the operators available in Excel.

SYMBOL	OPERATION
Unary Mathematical Operators	
–	Negation
()	Negation, in a cell only, not in a formula
%	Percent (operates on the value to its left)
Binary Mathematical Operators	
+	Addition
–	Subtraction
*	Multiplication
/	Division
^	Exponentiation
String Operator	
&	Concatenation
Logical Operators	
=	Equals
<	Less than
	Greater than
<=	Less than or equal to
=	Greater than or equal to
<>	Not equal to

Table 2.1: Operators available in Excel

Mathematical Operators The mathematical operators consist of the standard set expected in any high-level computer language. The unary operators are percent and negation. The % (percent) operator divides the number to its left by 100 and is equivalent to /100. Surrounding parentheses, as in (*number*), indicate negation in a cell entry, but not in a formula, where parentheses are used as separators. There is no + unary operator, since a positive value is assumed if no negation operator is present. If you insert one, Excel will remove it from your values and equations.

The binary operators are addition, subtraction, multiplication, division and exponentiation. All of them operate according to the familiar rules of arithmetic.

String Operators There is one string operator, concatenation, which is used to join two strings.

Logical Operators The logical operators are used to compare two numerical values or strings. The result of the operation is a value of TRUE or FALSE. When strings are compared, the case (upper or lower) of the characters is ignored. Use the EXACT() function to also compare the case of characters in strings.

Precedence The precedence of the operators determines how a formula is evaluated, that is, the order in which the operations will be performed. If you are not sure how a formula will be evaluated, use parentheses to force the correct order of evaluation. Table 2.2 lists the precedence of the operators. In any calculation, the operators at the top of the table are executed first, then the next highest operator, and so on.

Worksheet Functions

The worksheet functions are the primary value-manipulating functions in Excel. The macro functions, by contrast, are command and action equivalents. The worksheet functions can be used on both the worksheet and the macro sheet. Table 2.3 lists all of the worksheet functions by type. A function consists of the function name, a left parenthesis, some arguments separated by commas, and a right parenthesis.

Depending on the function, the required arguments can be numbers, logical values, strings, or cell references. If the required argument is a number, logical value, or string, you can usually use a cell reference or formula that evaluates to the correct type. If the argument is not of the correct type, Excel will attempt to convert it if possible. For example, the formula **=1+“1”** evaluates to the number 2, and **=1&“1”** evaluates to the string “11”. Formulas as arguments to functions can have a nesting of functions seven levels deep.

In these descriptions, the function name will be listed in uppercase letters and the arguments in italics surrounded by left and right angle brackets (<>). Arguments that can be omitted will also be surrounded with square brackets ([ ]). When you use these functions, they can be entered in either upper- or lowercase, because EXCEL does not distinguish between the two.

You can also code functions as macros and call them in the same way as predefined functions. While these functions will not be as fast as the built-in functions, they can be coded to calculate just about anything. See the DEFINE.NAME( ) macro function for more information.

SYMBOL	OPERATION
–	Negation
%	Percent
^	Exponentiation
* or /	Multiplication or division
+ or –	Addition or subtraction
&	Concatenation
= < > <= >= <>	Logical comparison

Table 2.2: Calculational precedence of the operators

NAME	DEFINITION
Math	
ABS()	Absolute value
FACT()	Factorial
INT()	Integer
MOD()	Modulus
RAND()	Random number
ROUND()	Round
SIGN()	Sign
SQRT()	Square root
TRUNC()	Truncate a number to an integer
Logarithmic	
EXP()	Exponential
LN()	Natural logarithm
LOG()	Log to any base
LOG10()	Common logarithm
Trigonometric	
ACOS()	Arccosine
ASIN()	Arcsine
ATAN()	Arctangent
ATAN2()	Arctangent (two input)
COS()	Cosine
PI()	The value π (3.1415926535898)
SIN()	Sine
TAN()	Tangent

Table 2.3: The worksheet functions by type

NAME	DEFINITION
Logical Values	
FALSE()	FALSE or 0
TRUE()	TRUE or 1
Logical Tests	
IF()	Logical branch IF
ISBLANK()	Test for a blank cell
ISERR()	Test for all errors but #N/A
ISERROR()	Test for all errors
ISLOGICAL()	Test for a logical value
ISNA()	Test for #N/A
ISNONTEXT()	Test for not a string
ISNUMBER()	Test for a number
ISREF()	Test for a cell reference
ISTEXT()	Test for a string
N()	Force a number
T()	Force a string
Boolean	
AND()	Logical AND
NOT()	Logical negation
OR()	Logical OR
String	
CHAR()	ASCII character from code
CLEAN()	Remove nonprintable characters
CODE()	ASCII code from character
DOLLAR()	Convert to currency format

Table 2.3: The worksheet functions by type (continued)

NAME	DEFINITION
String (continued)	
EXACT()	Exact string comparison
FIND()	Locate a substring
FIXED()	Convert to fixed format
INDIRECT()	Convert a string to a reference
LEFT()	Left side of a string
LEN()	Length of a string
LOWER()	Change to lower case
MID()	Extract part of a string
PROPER()	Capitalize first characters of words
REPLACE()	Replace a substring
REPT()	Repeat a string
RIGHT()	Right side of a string
SEARCH()	Search for a substring
SUBSTITUTE()	Replace a substring
TEXT()	Convert a number to a string
TRIM()	Remove redundant spaces
UPPER()	Convert to uppercase
VALUE()	Convert a string to a number
Date	
DATE()	Convert a date to a *serial day number*
DATEVALUE()	Convert a date to a *serial day number*
DAY()	The day from a *serial day number*
MONTH()	The month from a *serial day number*
NOW()	Today's date and time

Table 2.3: The worksheet functions by type (continued)

NAME	DEFINITION
Date (continued)	
WEEKDAY()	The weekday from a *serial day number*
YEAR()	The year from a *serial day number*
Time	
HOUR()	The hour from a *serial day number*
MINUTE()	A minute from a *serial day number*
SECOND()	A second from a *serial day number*
TIME()	Convert to a *serialal day number*
TIMEVALUE()	Convert to a *serial day number*
Basic Statistics	
AVERAGE()	Average some numbers
COUNT()	Count cells with numbers
COUNTA()	Count all cells
MAX()	Find the largest value
MIN()	Find the smallest value
PRODUCT()	Product of some numbers
STDEV()	Sample standard deviation
STDEVP()	Population standard deviation
SUM()	Sum some numbers
VAR()	Sample variance
VARP()	Population variance
Linear Curve Fit	
LINEST()	Linear curve coefficients
TREND()	Linear curve

Table 2.3: The worksheet functions by type (continued)

NAME	DEFINITION
Logarithmic Curve Fit	
GROWTH()	Growth curve
LOGEST()	Growth curve coefficients
Database	
DAVERAGE()	Average
DCOUNT()	Count values
DCOUNTA()	Count cells
DPRODUCT()	Product
DSUM()	Sum
DMAX()	Maximum value
DMIN()	Minimum value
DSTDEV()	Sample standard deviation
DSTDEVP()	Population standard deviation
DVAR()	Sample variance
DVARP()	Population variance
Investment Analysis	
FV()	Future value
IPMT()	Interest paid at a period
IRR()	Internal rate of return
MIRR()	Modified internal rate of return
NPER()	Number of periods
NPV()	Net present value
PMT()	Payment
PPMT()	Principle paid at a period

Table 2.3: The worksheet functions by type (continued)

NAME	DEFINITION
Investment Analysis (continued)	
PV()	Present value
RATE()	Interest rate
Depreciation	
DDB()	Double-declining-balance method
SLN()	Straight-line method
SYD()	Sum-of-the-years'-digits method
Table Lookup	
CHOOSE()	Choose a value from a list
HLOOKUP()	Horizontal table lookup
INDEX()	Extract a value from an array
LOOKUP()	Vector or table lookup
MATCH()	Exact vector lookup
VLOOKUP()	Vertical table lookup
Reference Characteristics	
AREAS()	The number of areas
CELL()	Info about a cell
COLUMN()	The column numbers
COLUMNS()	The number of columns
ROW()	The row numbers
ROWS()	The number of rows
TYPE()	The type of a value

Table 2.3: The worksheet functions by type (continued)

NAME	DEFINITION
Matrix	
MDETERM()	Determinant of a matrix
MINVERSE()	Matrix inverse
MMULT()	Matrix multiply
TRANSPOSE()	Matrix transpose
Error Value	
NA()	Not available

Table 2.3: The worksheet functions by type (continued)

ABS()

v: **ALL**

SYNTAX

ABS(<*number*>**)**

USAGE

ABS() returns the absolute value of its numeric argument.

SEE ALSO

SIGN()

ACOS()

v: **ALL**

SYNTAX

ACOS(<*number*>**)**

USAGE

The ACOS() function returns the arccosine of its argument—that is, the angle in radians whose cosine is <*number*> (<*number*>

must be in the range –1 to 1). The result is in the range 0 to π. If you need the result in degrees, multiply it by 180/PI().

SEE ALSO

ASIN(), ATAN(), ATAN2(), COS(), PI(), SIN(), TAN()

AND()

***v:* ALL**

SYNTAX

AND(<*logical_1*>[,<*logical_2*>[,...]])

USAGE

AND() returns the logical AND of its argument list. That is, if all of the arguments have the logical value TRUE, AND() returns TRUE. If any argument is FALSE, AND() returns FALSE.

AND() also responds to numbers. A value of 0 is equivalent to FALSE, while any non-zero value is equivalent to TRUE.

SEE ALSO

OR(), NOT()

AREAS()

v: **ALL**

SYNTAX

AREAS(<*reference*>**)**

USAGE

Unique to Excel is the ability to include nonrectangular and unconnected areas of the worksheet in a cell reference. The AREAS() function breaks down a reference and returns the number of distinct areas in it. Areas are defined as continuous, rectangular regions on the worksheet. Most cell references consist of only one area. However, if you hold down the Command key while selecting cells, you can select several unconnected areas, and make them part of the same cell reference. When typing a cell reference, separate the unconnected areas by commas, and surround the whole reference with parentheses. For example, the formula **=AREAS((A1:D9,E2:F10))** returns the number 2.

ASIN()

v: **ALL**

SYNTAX

ASIN(<*number*>**)**

USAGE

ASIN() returns the arcsine of its argument—that is, the angle in radians whose sine is *<number>* (*<number>* must be in the range –1 to 1). The result is in the range $-\pi/2$ to $\pi/2$. If you need the result in degrees, multiply it by 180/PI().

SEE ALSO

ACOS(), ATAN(), ATAN2(), COS(), PI(), SIN(), TAN()

ATAN() and ATAN2()

v: **ALL**

SYNTAX

ATAN(<*number*>**)**
ATAN2(<*x_number*>**,**<*y_number*>**)**

USAGE

ATAN() returns the arctangent in radians of the argument *<number>*—that is, the angle whose tangent is *<number>*. The result will be in the range $-\pi/2$ to $\pi/2$. If you need the result in degrees, multiply it by 180/PI().

The arctangent is a multivalued function, with equivalent values differing by π. If you know the numerator and denominator of the fraction that defines the tangent, you can use the second form of the function to determine which one is correct. The ATAN2() function returns the arctangent of the quotient *<y_number/<x_number>*, with the result in the range $-\pi$ to π.

SEE ALSO

ASIN(), ACOS(), COS(), PI(), SIN(), TAN()

AVERAGE()

***v:* ALL**

SYNTAX

AVERAGE(<*numbers_1*>[,<*numbers_2*>[,...]])

USAGE

AVERAGE(), which is equivalent to SUM()/COUNT(), calculates and returns the average of all of the numbers contained in its arguments. It can have up to 14 arguments, any of which can be references to arrays of cells. Any referenced cells that are blank or contain logical values, or strings will be ignored. This feature allows you to average across blank lines and column headings without them being included in the average.

SEE ALSO

COUNT(), DAVERAGE(), MAX(), MIN(), PRODUCT(), STDEV(), SUM(), VAR()

CELL()

v: **1.5**

SYNTAX

CELL(*<string>*[,*<reference>*])

USAGE

CELL() examines a cell and its contents and returns a value depending on the information being requested with *<string>*. There are nine possible values of *<string>*, and nine different results for the function. (Quotation marks are required if you type the string into the function, but not if the argument is a formula or cell reference.)

"width"	returns the integer column width of the cell, measured in character widths of the currently selected font.
"row"	returns the row number of the cell.
"col"	returns the column number of the cell. If you need the column letter rather than the number, use the expression: **CHAR(CELL("col",*<reference>*)+64)**.
"protect"	returns 1 if a cell is protected (locked); otherwise, it returns 0.
"address"	returns the cell reference as a string. The returned reference will be an absolute reference, even if *<reference>* is a relative reference.
"contents"	returns the contents of the cell. This is the same as just typing a cell reference in a formula.

"format"	returns the numeric format of the cell as set with the Format Number command. The format is returned as a code in a text string. See the **FORMAT.NUMBER()** macro function for a list of the formats and codes.
"prefix"	returns the justification of the text in a cell as a code in a string. The possible values are " ' " single quote (left justified), "^" caret (centered), " " " double quote (right justified), and " " blank (no text in the cell).
"type"	returns the type of the cell contents as a code in a text string. The possible values are "b" (blank), "l" (label), and "v" (number).

If *<reference>* is omitted on the worksheet, the function examines itself. If it is omitted on the macro sheet, CELL() examines the currently active selection. If it consists of more than one cell, the one in the upper-left corner of the reference is used.

SEE ALSO

AREAS(), COLUMN(), COLUMNS(), ROW(), ROWS(), INDIRECT(), ISBLANK(), ISERR(), ISERROR(), ISLOGICAL(), ISNA(), ISNONTEXT(), ISNUMBER(), ISREF(), ISTEXT(), N(), T(), TYPE()

CHAR()

v: **1.5**

SYNTAX

CHAR(<*ascii_code*>)

USAGE

CHAR() returns a single ASCII character that corresponds to the <*ascii_code*> (1 through 255) given as its argument. Codes 1 through 31 are control codes. Codes 32 through 127 are the standard typewriter characters. Codes 128 through 255 are the extended characters, which depend on the font and machine being used. Any codes that lack a symbol, or that do not cause an action to take place are marked with the missing-character symbol (a square for most fonts).

The table inside the back cover shows the codes for the Geneva font. Some of the action-taking codes are 9 (Tab), 13 (Carriage Return), and 202 (nonbreaking space).

The CHAR() function is the inverse of the CODE() function.

SEE ALSO

CODE()

CHOOSE()

v: **ALL**

SYNTAX

CHOOSE(<*index*>,<*value_1*>[,<*value_2*>[,...]])

USAGE

CHOOSE() uses the value of the variable <*index*> to select and return one of the values in the list after it. If <*index*> equals 1, the function will return <*value_1*>, if <*index*> equals 2, the function will return <*value_2*>, and so forth. If <*index*> is zero or greater than the number of values in the list, the function returns the error value #VALUE!.

SEE ALSO

INDEX(), HLOOKUP(), VLOOKUP()

CLEAN()

v: **ALL**

SYNTAX

CLEAN(<*string*>)

USAGE

CLEAN() returns *<string>* after removing any ASCII characters with codes less than 32. This range includes nearly all of the nonprinting characters.

SEE ALSO

LEFT(), MID(), RIGHT(), REPLACE(), SEARCH(), SUBSTITUTE(), TRIM()

CODE()

v: **1.5**

SYNTAX

CODE(*<string>***)**

USAGE

The CODE() function returns the ASCII code for the first character in *<string>*. See the **CHAR()** function for information about ASCII codes.

The CODE() function is the inverse of the CHAR() function.

SEE ALSO

CHAR()

COLUMN()

v: **ALL**

SYNTAX

COLUMN([<*reference*>]**)**

USAGE

The COLUMN() function returns the column number of the cell reference if the reference is to a single cell or column of cells. If the cell reference contains more than one column, COLUMN() returns a horizontal array of column numbers, one for each column in the cell reference. To output the array, select a horizontal group of cells, large enough to contain the array. Put the COLUMN() command in the leftmost cell and hold down the Command key when pressing Enter or clicking the check mark. (See the section on arrays in the Introduction.)

SEE ALSO

ROW()

COLUMNS()

v: ALL

SYNTAX

COLUMNS(*<array>*)

USAGE

COLUMNS() returns the number of columns in the array or cell reference.

SEE ALSO

ROWS()

COS()

v: ALL

SYNTAX

COS(*<angle>*)

USAGE

COS() calculates the cosine of an angle. The angle must be in radians. The result is in the range –1 to 1. If the angle is in degrees, multiply it by PI()/180 to convert it into radians.

SEE ALSO

ASIN(), ACOS(), ATAN(), ATAN2(), PI(), SIN(), TAN()

COUNT() and COUNTA()

***v*: 1.5**

SYNTAX

```
COUNT(<values_1>[,<values_2>[,<...>]])
COUNTA(<values_1>[,<values_2>[,<...>]])
```

USAGE

The COUNT() function counts the number of numeric values in the arguments. Any cells that are blank, or contain logical values or text will be ignored. This feature allows you to count across blank lines and column headings without them being included in the average.

The COUNTA() function counts all of the values in the arguments, ignoring only blank cells.

While there can be only 14 arguments in these functions, any one of them can be a reference to many cells.

SEE ALSO

AVERAGE(), DCOUNT(), MAX(), MIN(), PRODUCT(), STDEV(), SUM(), VAR()

DATE() and DATEVALUE()

v: **1.5**

SYNTAX

DATE(<*year*>,<*month*>,<*day*>**)**
DATEVALUE(<*date_string*>**)**

USAGE

DATE() and DATEVALUE() are used to convert a date into a *serial day number.*

These functions are not often needed, because Excel automatically converts text you type in date format into a *serial day number.* Use the DATE() function where the day, month and year are in separate cells, or are the result of formulas. If the date is part of a formula, you can either use the DATE() function or just put the date, in standard date format, in quotes. Standard date formats are 8/6/88 and 6-Aug-88. The slash and hyphen separators are interchangeable. The DATEVALUE() function can be used to extract the date from a string that contains a date and a time.

<*year*> must be in the range 1904 to 2040, or equivalently 4 to 140. <*month*> must be in the range 1 to 12. <*day*> must be in the range 1 to 28 or 31, depending on the month. <*date_string*> may be in any of Excel's date formats. If the year is omitted, the current year is used. See the Introduction for more information on dates.

SEE ALSO

DAY(), HOUR(), MINUTE(), MONTH(), NOW(), SECOND(), TIME(), TIMEVALUE(), WEEKDAY(), YEAR()

DAVERAGE()

v: **ALL**

SYNTAX

DAVERAGE(<*database*>,<*field*>,<*criteria*>**)**

USAGE

DAVERAGE() is the database analog of the AVERAGE() function. Rather than averaging all of the cells in a column, it will average only those cells with specific contents in adjacent columns. That is, it searches the records of a database for matches to the criteria and then averages the numbers in the specified field. See the Introduction for a description and syntax of database and criteria ranges. As with the AVERAGE() function, blank cells and cells containing strings or logical values will not be included.

The argument <*database*> must reference a valid database, but need not be a database defined with the Options Set Database command. It can be referenced with a standard cell reference, or named range. If you use the name *database*, the database defined with the Options Set Database command will be used. The same applies to the <*criteria*> argument. It need not be the criteria defined with the Options Set Criteria command, but can be any valid criteria range. If you use the name *criteria*, the criteria defined with the Options Set Criteria command will be used. The <*field*> argument must be either a string or number. If it is a string, it must contain the field name of the column. If it is a number, it must be the column number of the database (the leftmost column is number 1).

SEE ALSO

AVERAGE(), DCOUNT(), DMAX(), DMIN(), DPRODUCT(), DSTDEV(), DSUM(), DVAR()

DAY()

***v:* ALL**

SYNTAX

DAY(<*serial_day_number*>**)**

USAGE

DAY() calculates the day of the month that corresponds to a <*serial_day_number*>.

This function is not needed to display complete dates, because Excel will automatically convert <*serial_day_numbers*> into dates if you format the cell as a date. Use this function where you need the number of the day of the month.

The function DAY() will ignore any fractional parts (time of day) of a <*serial_day_number*>.

SEE ALSO

DATE(), DATEVALUE(), HOUR(), MINUTE(), MONTH(), NOW(), SECOND(), TIME(), TIMEVALUE(), WEEKDAY(), YEAR()

DCOUNT() and DCOUNTA()

v: **1.5**

SYNTAX

DCOUNT(<*database*>**,**<*field*>**,**<*criteria*>**)**
DCOUNTA(<*database*>**,**<*field*>**,**<*criteria*>**)**

USAGE

DCOUNT() and DCOUNTA() are the database analogs of the COUNT() and COUNTA() functions. Rather than counting all of the cells in a column, they count only those cells with specific contents in adjacent columns. That is, they search the records of a database for matches to the criteria, and then count the numbers in the specified field. See the Introduction for a description and syntax of database and criteria ranges. The DCOUNT() function will ignore blank cells and cells containing strings or logical values. The DCOUNTA() function will ignore blank cells. See the DAVERAGE() function for a discussion of the arguments.

SEE ALSO

COUNT(), DAVERAGE(), DMAX(), DMIN(), DPRODUCT(), DSTDEV(), DSUM(), DVAR()

DDB()

v: 1.5

SYNTAX

DDB(<*cost*>,<*salvage_value*>,<*life*>,<*current_period*>**)**

USAGE

DDB() calculates the depreciation of an asset at a specific period in its lifetime, using the double-declining-balance method—an accelerated depreciation method that uses double the straight-line depreciation percentage, applied each period to the remaining balance. It uses the smaller of these two expressions: (<*cost*>–<*depreciation_from_previous_periods*>)*2/<*life*>, or (<*cost*>–<*salvage_value*>)). The <*cost*> is the original cost of the asset. The <*salvage value*> is the value of the asset at the end of its lifetime. The <*life*> argument is the lifetime of the asset, and the <*current period*> is the period at which you want to know the depreciation.

Note that <*life*> and <*current_ period*> must be in the same units (months, years, and so forth).

SEE ALSO

SLN(), SYD()

DMAX()

v: **ALL**

SYNTAX

DMAX(<*database*>**,**<*field*>**,**<*criteria*>**)**

USAGE

DMAX() is the database analog of the MAX() function. It searches the records of a database for matches to <*criteria*>, and then finds the record with the largest value in the specified field. See the Introduction for a description and syntax of database and criteria ranges. Blank cells, and cells containing strings or logical values will not be searched. See **DAVERAGE()** for a description of the arguments.

SEE ALSO

DAVERAGE(), DCOUNT(), DMIN(), DPRODUCT(), DSTDEV(), DSUM(), DVAR(), MAX()

DMIN()

v: **ALL**

SYNTAX

DMIN(<*database*>,<*field*>,<*criteria*>**)**

USAGE

DMIN() is the database analog of the MIN() function. It searches the records of a database for matches to <*criteria*>, and then finds the record with the smallest value in the specified field. See the Introduction for a description and syntax of database and criteria ranges. Blank cells, and cells containing strings or logical values will not be searched. See **DAVERAGE()** for a description of the arguments.

SEE ALSO

DAVERAGE(), DCOUNT(), DMAX(), DPRODUCT(), DSTDEV(), DSUM(), DVAR(), MIN()

DOLLAR()

v: **ALL**

SYNTAX

DOLLAR(<*number*>[,<*number_of_digits*>]**)**

USAGE

DOLLAR() rounds a number to <*number_of_digits*> and converts it to a string in currency format. A dollar sign is placed at the beginning, and commas are inserted after every third digit. Negative numbers are enclosed in parentheses. If <*number_of_digits*> is omitted, 2 is assumed. If it is negative, rounding occurs to the left of the decimal.

SEE ALSO

FIXED(), TEXT(), VALUE(), ROUND()

DPRODUCT()

v: **1.5**

SYNTAX

DPRODUCT(<*database*>,<*field*>,<*criteria*>**)**

USAGE

DPRODUCT() searches the records of a database for matches to *<criteria>*, and then calculates the product of the numbers in the specified field of those records. See the Introduction for a description and syntax of database and criteria ranges. Blank cells and cells containing strings or logical values will not be included. See the DAVERAGE() function for a description of the arguments.

SEE ALSO

DAVERAGE(), DCOUNT(), DCOUNTA(), DMAX(), DMIN(), DSTDEV(), DSTDEVP(), DSUM(), DVAR(), DVARP(), PRODUCT()

DSTDEV() and DSTDEVP()

v: **1.5**

SYNTAX

DSTDEV(*<database>*,*<field>*,*<criteria>***)**
DSTDEVP(*<database >*,*<field>*,*<criteria>***)**

USAGE

DSTDEV() is the database analog of the STDEV() function. It uses only those cells with specific contents in adjacent columns. That is, it searches the records of a database for matches to *<criteria>*, and then calculates the sample standard deviation of the numbers in the specified field. See the Introduction for a description and syntax of database and criteria ranges. Blank cells, and cells containing strings or logical values will not be included.

The DSTDEVP() function works in the same way as the DSTDEV() function, except that it calculates the true population standard deviation. It is the database analog of the STDEVP() function. See the DAVERAGE() function for a description of the arguments, and the STDEV() function for a description of the equations used.

SEE ALSO

DAVERAGE(), DCOUNT(), DMAX(), DMIN(), DPRODUCT(), DSUM(), DVAR(), STDEV()

DSUM()

v: **ALL**

SYNTAX

DSUM(<*database*>,<*field*>,<*criteria*>**)**

USAGE

DSUM() is the database analog of the SUM() function. It searches the records of <*database*> for matches to <*criteria*>, and then totals the numbers in the specified <*field*>. See the Introduction for a description and syntax of database and criteria ranges. Blank cells, and cells containing strings or logical values will not be included. See **DAVERAGE()** for a description of the arguments.

SEE ALSO

DAVERAGE(), DCOUNT(), DMAX(), DMIN(), DPROD-UCT(), DSTDEV(), DVAR(), SUM()

DVAR() and DVARP()

v: **1.5**

SYNTAX

DVAR(<*database*>,<*field*>,<*criteria*>**)**
DVARP(<*database* >,<*field*>,<*criteria*>**)**

USAGE

DVAR() is the database analog of the VAR() function. It searches the records of a database for matches to the *<criteria>*, and then calculates the sample variance of the numbers in the specified field. See the Introduction for a description and syntax of a database range and a criteria range. Blank cells, and cells containing strings or logical values will not be included.

The DVARP() function works in the same way as the DVAR() function, except that it calculates the true population variance. See **DAVERAGE()** for a description of the arguments, and **STDEV()** for a description of the equations used.

SEE ALSO

DAVERAGE(), DCOUNT(), DMAX(), DMIN(), DPROD-UCT(), DSTDEV(), DSUM(), VAR()

EXACT()

v: **1.5**

SYNTAX

EXACT(<*string_1*>,<*string_2*>**)**

USAGE

EXACT() is used to see if two strings are exactly equal. The function will return the logical value TRUE if they are exactly the same, including capitalization of letters; otherwise it will return FALSE. The expression (<*string_1*>=<*string_2*>) also compares two strings, but ignores capitalization. Note that the expression and the function both compare all of the characters in the strings, including leading and trailing blanks and nonprinting characters (see **CHAR()**).

SEE ALSO

FIND(), LEN(), SEARCH()

SYNTAX

EXP(*<number>***)**

USAGE

The EXP() function calculates **e** raised to the power of the argument *<number>*, where **e** is the base of the natural logarithms, 2.718281828459.... While in theory *<number>* can be any number, values greater than 709 cause numeric overflow and the #NUM! error will result. Likewise, for arguments less than –708 the function will return a value of 0. EXP() is the inverse of the LN() function, the natural logarithm. (To calculate powers of bases other than **e**, use the exponentiation operation, *<base>*^*<number>*.)

SEE ALSO

LN(), LOG(), LOG10()

FACT()

v: 1.5

SYNTAX

FACT(<*number*>)

USAGE

FACT() calculates the factorial (*n*!) of a number. The factorial is defined as

$$n! = n(n-1)(n-2)...(2)(1)$$

with the factorial of 0 defined as 1. While the argument can theoretically have any positive integer value, arguments greater than 170 will cause numeric overflow.

FALSE()

v: ALL

SYNTAX

FALSE()

USAGE

The FALSE() function returns the logical value FALSE. You do not need to use this function to get the value FALSE. Simply type the word **FALSE** where it is needed, and Excel will interpret it as the logical value rather than the text string "FALSE". To get a text string in a cell rather than the logical value, put it in quotes and preface it with an equal sign. This function is included mainly for compatibility with Lotus 1-2-3.

SEE ALSO

TRUE()

FIND()

v: **1.5**

SYNTAX

FIND(<*search_string*>,<*target_string*>[,<*starting_position*>]**)**

USAGE

The FIND() function returns the character position in <*target_string*> of the first character of the first occurrence of <*search_string*> that it finds. The search, which is case sensitive, begins at character position <*starting_position*> in <*target_string*> and continues left to right. (The first character in the string is position number 1.) If it is omitted, 1 is assumed. If the string is not found, or <*starting_position*> is less than 1 or greater than the length of <*target_string*>, the error value

#VALUE! is returned. If <*search_string*> is null (""), <*starting_position*> will be returned.

SEE ALSO

EXACT(), LEN(), SEARCH()

FIXED()

v: **ALL**

SYNTAX

FIXED(<*number*>**[,**<*decimals*>**])**

USAGE

The FIXED() function rounds a number to <*decimals*> digits, and then converts it to a text string with a comma after every third digit left of the decimal point. If <*decimals*> is omitted, 2 is assumed; negative values round to the left of the decimal.

SEE ALSO

DOLLAR(), ROUND(), TEXT()

FV()

v: **ALL**

SYNTAX

FV(<*rate*>,<*periods*>,<*payment*>,<*present_value*>[,<*type*>]**)**

USAGE

FV() calculates the future value of an annuity, which is a periodic cash flow of equal amounts in an interest-bearing account. The future value of an annuity is its value after <*periods*> payments, given its initial or present value, the amount of the periodic payments, and the interest rate. Use cash-flow conventions to determine the sign of the dollar values. Cash received is positive and cash paid out is negative. There are two types of annuities. Type 0 annuities are ordinary annuities, with the payment at the end of the period. Type 1 annuities have the payment at the beginning of the period. If <*type*> is omitted, 0 is assumed.

All of the financial functions are calculated by solving one of the following two equations. The first equation is used when *rate* is not equal to zero, and the second is used when *rate* is equal to zero.

$$pv(1+rate)^{periods} + pmt(1+rate*type)\left(\frac{(1+rate)^{periods}-1}{rate}\right)+fv=0$$

$$pv+pmt*periods+fv=0$$

where *pv* is the present value of the annuity, *rate* is the interest rate per period as a fraction (not a percent), *periods* is the number of periods, *pmt* is the amount of a periodic payment, *fv* is the future value of the annuity, and *type* is the type of annuity (0 or 1).

SEE ALSO

IPMT(), IRR(), MIRR(), NPER(), NPV(), PMT(), PPMT(), PV(), RATE()

GROWTH()

v: **ALL**

SYNTAX

GROWTH(<*array_y*>**[,**<*array_x*>**[,**<*array_x2*>**]])**

USAGE

GROWTH() uses regression techniques to calculate a curve fit of the exponential growth curve ($y = b*m^x$) to the <*array_x*> and <*array_y*> data. The exponential growth curve is calculated in the same manner as is used for the LOGEST() function. The <*array_x2*> data, or the <*array_x*> data if the <*array_x2*> data is omitted, is then inserted into the exponential growth curve equation and a new array of *y* data is returned. This function returns an array the same size as <*array_x2*> or <*array_x*>, so you must select an area of the appropriate size on the worksheet, and insert the function into all of the cells by holding down the Command key when pressing Return or clicking the check mark.

The <*array_x*> and <*array_y*> arrays must both be the same size, because the values in these arrays are assumed to correspond one for one.

SEE ALSO

LINEST(), LOGEST(), TREND()

HLOOKUP()

v: **ALL**

SYNTAX

HLOOKUP(<*lookup_value*>**,**<*search_array*>**,**<*row_index*>**)**

USAGE

HLOOKUP() searches the first row of <*search_array*> left to right for the largest value that is less than or equal to <*lookup_value*>. It then moves down to the row specified by <*row_index*>, and returns the contents of the cell found there. The contents of the first row can be either values or text and must be in ascending order, with numbers < text < logicals. If <*row_index*> is less than 1, the error value #VALUE! will be returned. If <*row_index*> is 1, then the contents of the cell on the first row will be returned. If <*row_index*> is greater than the number of rows in <*search_array*>, the function will return the error value #REF!. If <*lookup_value*> is less than the first value in the first row, the function will return the error value #N/A.

SEE ALSO

INDEX(), LOOKUP(), MATCH(), VLOOKUP()

HOUR()

v: **ALL**

SYNTAX

HOUR(<*serial_day_number*>**)**

USAGE

HOUR() extracts the hour from the <*serial_day_number*>, which is the number of days between a date and January 1, 1904, including January 1, 1904, plus the time as a fractional part of a day. That is, 0 is midnight, 0.5 is noon, and so forth. The HOUR() function is not needed to display a time, as Excel will do this automatically if you format a cell as a time. This function ignores any integer parts (dates) of its argument. See the Introduction for more information on dates and times.

SEE ALSO

DATE(), DAY(), MINUTE(), MONTH(), NOW(), SECOND(), TIME(), WEEKDAY(), YEAR()

IF()

v: **ALL**

SYNTAX

IF(<*logical_test*>**,**<*return_if_true*>**[[,**<*return_if_false*>**])**

USAGE

IF() evaluates <*logical_test*>. If it is TRUE, the function returns the <*return_if_true*> value. If it is FALSE, the function returns <*return_if_false*>. Either return value can be a number, string, logical, or formula. Use this function to select alternate values or calculations, depending on a test that returns a logical value. It is also useful for trapping error values.

SEE ALSO

ISBLANK(), ISERR(), ISERROR(), ISLOGICAL(), ISNA(), ISNONTEXT(), ISNUMBER(), ISREF(), ISTEXT()

INDEX()

v: **ALL**

SYNTAX

INDEX(<*reference*>**,**<*row*>**[,**<*column* >**[,**<*area*>**]])**

USAGE

INDEX() returns the reference or value of a cell in a vector, array or multiarea array. Whether the reference or value is returned is determined by the context of the function in a formula. The <*area*> argument selects the area in the reference. (See **AREA()** for a discussion of areas.) In most cases you will have only one area, so <*area*> can be omitted. The <*row*> and <*column*> numbers select the cell within a particular <*area*> of the <*reference*>. If the <*reference*> consists of a single vector, only one <*row*> or <*column*> number is needed to select the cell.

SEE ALSO

HLOOKUP(), LOOKUP(), MATCH(), VLOOKUP()

INDIRECT()

v: **1.5**

SYNTAX

INDIRECT(<*reference*>**,**<*reference_type*>**)**

USAGE

INDIRECT() returns the reference to the cell contained in <*reference*>. The cell <*reference*> must contain a string representation of a cell reference, or a formula that evaluates to a string. If <*reference_type*> is TRUE, the string representation of the reference must be in the A1 style of cell referencing. If it is FALSE, the reference must be in the RICI style. See the Introduction for more information about cell referencing.

INT()

v: **ALL**

SYNTAX

INT(<*number*>)

USAGE

INT() returns the largest integer that is less than or equal to <*number*>. This function behaves as expected for positive numbers by just stripping off the fractional part of a number. For negative numbers, it follows the definition above. For example, while **=INT(5.6)** returns 5, **=INT (–5.6)** returns –6. To strip the fractional part of any number, use TRUNC(). This would truncate, for example, –5.6 to –5. Note that the Lotus 1-2-3 INT() function is equivalent to the Excel TRUNC() function. The difference will be apparent only for negative numbers.

SEE ALSO

MOD(), ROUND(), TRUNC(), VALUE()

IPMT()

v: 1.5

SYNTAX

IPMT(<*rate*>**,**<*period*>**,**<*periods* >**,**<*present_value*>**,**
[<*future_value*>**],[**<*type*>**])**

USAGE

IPMT() calculates the part of a periodic payment of an annuity that is interest, as opposed to the part that is principle (see **PPMT()**), at some point during the lifetime of the annuity. The IPMT() function calculates the interest payment at <*period*> by calculating the future value of a partially paid annuity, and then multiplying that by the interest rate. See **FV()** for more information about annuity functions, and the arguments.

SEE ALSO

FV(), IRR(), MIRR(), NPER(), NPV(), PMT(), PPMT(), PV(), RATE()

IRR()

v: ALL

SYNTAX

IRR(<*cash_flows*>[,<*guess*>])

USAGE

IRR() calculates the internal rate of return, or discount rate for a series of irregular cash flows. The internal rate of return is the effective interest rate of a series of cash flows—the interest rate that gives the series of cash flows a net present value (see **NPV()**) of zero.

Since the first cash flow is usually negative (the investment) and the rest are positive (the returns on the investment), the internal rate of return is the interest rate at which the present value of the returns on the investment is equal to the original investment.

While the cash flows are of irregular size, they are assumed to take place at regular intervals. Also, any cash flows received are assumed to be reinvested at the calculated rate. The solution is found iteratively, using <*guess*> as a starting point. The closer <*guess*> is to the correct rate, the faster the iteration will converge. Use cash flow conventions to determine the sign of the dollar values. Cash received is positive and cash paid out is negative.

If the iteration process does not converge after 20 iterations, IRR() will return the value #NUM!. If this happens, try a different value for <*guess*>.

Use this function with caution if you have negative cash flows other than the first one. The internal rate of return is known to be a poor indicator of investment returns in this case.

SEE ALSO

FV(), IPMT(), IRR(), MIRR(), NPER(), NPV(), PMT(), PPMT(), PV()

ISx()

v: **See below**

SYNTAX

ISBLANK(<*value*>**)***
ISERR(<*value*>**)***
ISERROR(<*value*>**)**
ISLOGICAL(<*value*>**)***
ISNA(<*value*>**)**
ISNONTEXT(<*value*>**)***
ISNUMBER(<*value*>**)***
ISREF(<*value*>**)**
ISTEXT(<*value*>**)***

* Version 1.5; others all versions

USAGE

These functions test the contents of their argument to see if it is of a particular type. If it is, they return TRUE; otherwise, they return FALSE. The primary use of these functions, combined with the IF() function, is to trap errors by testing the arguments, or results of a calculation.

ISBLANK() tests to see if a cell is blank. Note that a cell containing a blank space (" ") is not a blank cell, rather it contains a string consisting of the space character.

ISERR() tests to see if a cell contains any error value except #N/A.

ISERROR() tests to see if a cell contains any error value (#N/A, #VALUE!, #REF!, #DIV/0!, #NUM!, #NAME?, #NULL!). See the Introduction for more information about error values.

ISLOGICAL() tests to see if a cell contains a logical value.

ISNA() tests to see if a cell contains the error value #N/A.

ISNONTEXT() tests to see if a cell does not contain text.

ISNUMBER() tests to see if a cell contains a number.

ISREF() tests to see if its argument is a reference or a formula that evaluates to a reference. If you try to test the contents of another cell by making *<value>* a reference to it, the function will always return TRUE, because it is testing *<value>* rather then the cell *<value>* references. You can test names to see if they are defined as cell references.

ISTEXT() tests to see if a cell contains a text string.

SEE ALSO

IF()

LEFT()

v: **1.5**

SYNTAX

LEFT(<*string*>[,<*number_of_characters*>]**)**

USAGE

LEFT() returns a string containing the leftmost <*number_of_characters*> from <*string*>. If <*number_of_characters*> is greater than the length of <*string*>, all of <*string*> is returned. (The second argument must be greater than 0. If it is omitted, 1 is assumed.)

SEE ALSO

CLEAN(), MID(), RIGHT(), REPLACE(), SEARCH(), SUBSTITUTE(), TRIM()

LEN()

v: **1.5**

SYNTAX

LEN(<*string*>**)**

USAGE

The LEN() function returns the number of characters in <*string*>.

LINEST()

v: **ALL**

SYNTAX

LINEST(<*array_y*>[,<*array_x*>]**)**

USAGE

LINEST() uses regression techniques to calculate a curve fit of the linear curve ($y = m*x + b$) to the <*array_x*> and <*array_y*> data. It then returns a two-cell horizontal array containing the coefficients *m* and *b*. Because it returns two values, you must select a two-cell, horizontal area on the worksheet, and insert the function into both cells by holding down the Command key when pressing Enter or clicking the check mark.

The <*array_x*> and <*array_y*> arrays must be the same size, because the values in these arrays are assumed to correspond one for one.

SEE ALSO

GROWTH(), LOGEST(), TREND()

LN(), LOG(), and LOG10()

v: ALL (LOG() V1.5)

SYNTAX

LN(<*number*>**)**
LOG(<*number*>[,<*base*>]**)**
LOG10(<*number*>**)**

USAGE

LN() returns the natural logarithm (base **e** = 2.71828...) of <*number*>.

The LOG() function returns the logarithm to the base <*base*> of <*number*>. It is equivalent to either: LN(<*number*>)/LN(<*base*>) or LOG10(<*number*>)/LOG10(<*base*>). The argument <*base*> must be greater than 0. If it is omitted, 10 is assumed.

The LOG10() function returns the common logarithm (base 10) of <*number*>.

Use the EXP() function to get the inverse of the LN() function. Use the power operator (^) to get the inverse of the logarithm to any other base. Note that on a Macintosh with a numeric coprocessor (Mac II), the logarithm functions will fail for numbers less than 2^{-65} (about 2.7×10^{-20}). This is a bug in version 1.5 that should be corrected in later versions.

SEE ALSO

EXP()

LOGEST()

***v*: ALL**

SYNTAX

LOGEST(<*array_y*>[,<*array_x*>]**)**

USAGE

The LOGEST() function uses regression techniques to calculate a curve fit of the exponential growth curve ($y = b*m^x$) to the <*array_x*> and <*array_y*> data. It then returns a two-cell horizontal array containing the coefficients *m* and *b*. Because it returns two values, you must select a two cell, horizontal area on the worksheet, and insert the function into both cells by holding down the Command key when pressing Enter or clicking the check mark.

The <*array_x*> and <*array_y*> arrays must be the same size, because the values in these arrays are assumed to correspond one for one. All of the values in <*array y*> must be positive.

SEE ALSO

GROWTH(), LINEST(), TREND()

LOOKUP()

***v:* ALL**

SYNTAX

LOOKUP(<*lookup_value*>**,**[<*search_array*>|<*search_vector*>][,<*result_vector*>])

USAGE

If the second argument is a vector, the LOOKUP() function searches <*search_vector*> for the largest value that is less than or equal to <*lookup_value*>. It then returns the contents of the corresponding cell in <*result_vector*>. The contents of the <*search_vector*> can be either values or text, and must be in ascending order, with numbers < text < logicals. If <*lookup_value*> is less than the first value in the first column, the function will return the error value #N/A.

If the second argument is an array, LOOKUP() will search along the first row or column of <*search_array*>, whichever has the most elements. If the array is square, the function will search the first column. It will then return the value in the last row or column that is in the same position as the cell found in the first row or column.

SEE ALSO

HLOOKUP(), VLOOKUP(), MATCH()

LOWER()

v: 1.5

SYNTAX

LOWER(<*string*>)

USAGE

LOWER() returns <*string*> with all characters converted to lowercase.

SEE ALSO

PROPER(), UPPER()

MATCH()

***v:* ALL**

SYNTAX

MATCH(<*lookup_value*>**,**<*search_vector*>**[,**<*comparison_type*>**])**

USAGE

MATCH() searches <*search_vector*> for a match to <*lookup_value*>. It then returns the cell number of the match. If no match is found, the function returns #N/A.

The contents of <*lookup_value*> and <*search_vector*> can be numbers, text, or logical values. The integer <*comparison_type*> determines how <*lookup_value*> is compared to <*search_vector*>. If <*comparison_type*> has a value of 1 or is omitted, MATCH() finds the largest value less than or equal to <*lookup_value*>, and <*search_vector*> must be in ascending order, with numbers < text < logicals. If <*comparison_type*> is 0, MATCH() finds the value that is equal to <*lookup_value*>. If <*comparison_type*> is –1, MATCH() finds the largest value greater than or equal to <*lookup_value*>, and <*search_vector*> must be in descending order. If <*lookup_value*> is text, the wildcard characters * and ? can be used. Wildcard characters work well only with <*comparison_type*> equal to 0, so do not use them with types 1 and –1.

SEE ALSO

HLOOKUP(), INDEX(), LOOKUP(), MATCH(), VLOOKUP()

MAX()

v: ALL

SYNTAX

MAX(<*values_1*>[,<*values_2*>[,...]])

USAGE

MAX() finds the maximum of the numbers in the arguments. Any cells that are blank or contain logical values or text are ignored. This feature allows you to search across blank lines and column headings without including them. If there are no numbers in the arguments, MAX() returns 0. There can be up to 14 arguments, any of which can be a reference to many cells.

SEE ALSO

AVERAGE(), COUNT(), DMAX(), MIN(), PRODUCT(), STDEV(), SUM(), VAR()

MDETERM()

v: 1.5

SYNTAX

MDETERM(<*array*>**)**

USAGE

MDETERM() returns the determinant of the matrix *<array>*. You can enter the argument as a square array or cell reference. If the matrix is not square, or if it contains blank cells, cells containing strings, or cells containing logical values, the function will return the error value #VALUE!.

SEE ALSO

MINVERSE(), MMULT(), TRANSPOSE()

MID()

v: **ALL**

SYNTAX

MID(*<string>***,***<start_character>***,***<characters>***)**

USAGE

MID() extracts and returns *<characters>* characters from *<string>*, starting at character number *<start_character>*. If *<characters>* plus *<start_character>* is greater than the length of the string, all of the characters from *<start_character>* to the end of the string are returned.

SEE ALSO

CLEAN(), LEFT(), MID(), RIGHT(), REPLACE(), SEARCH(), SUBSTITUTE(), TRIM()

MIN()

v: **ALL**

SYNTAX

MIN(<*values_1*>[,<*values_2*>[,...]]**)**

USAGE

MIN() finds the minimum of one or more sets of numbers. Any cells that are blank or contain logical values or text will be ignored. This feature allows you to search across blank lines and column headings without including them. If there are no numbers in the arguments, MIN() returns 0. There can be up to 14 arguments, any of which can be a reference to many cells.

SEE ALSO

AVERAGE(), COUNT(), DMIN(), MAX(), PRODUCT(), STDEV(), SUM(), VAR()

MINUTE()

v: **ALL**

SYNTAX

MINUTE(<*serial_day_number*>**)**

USAGE

MINUTE() extracts the minute from the <*serial_day_number*>, ignoring any integer parts (dates). MINUTE() is not needed to display a time, as Excel will do this automatically if you format a cell as a time. See the Introduction for more information on dates and times.

SEE ALSO

DATE(), DAY(), HOUR(), MONTH(), NOW(), SECOND(), TIME(), WEEKDAY(), YEAR()

MINVERSE()

v: **1.5**

SYNTAX

MINVERSE(<*array*>**)**

USAGE

MINVERSE() returns the inverse of the matrix *<array>*. Since it returns a matrix, you must select an array of cells the same size as the argument matrix and insert the function into all of those cells by holding down the Command key when pressing Enter or clicking the check mark. If the matrix is not square, or if it contains blank cells, cells containing strings, or cells containing logical values, the function will return the error value #VALUE!. Beware of inverting large matrices (greater than 50 × 50), because they can cause a system crash with Version 1.5 of Excel.

If the determinant of a matrix, calculated with the MDETERM() function, is small compared to the numbers in the matrix, then the matrix is probably singular. MINVERSE() may be able to invert the matrix but the results will be garbage.

SEE ALSO

MDETERM(), MMULT(), TRANSPOSE()

MIRR()

v: **ALL**

SYNTAX

MIRR(*<cash_flows>*,*<finance_rate>*,*<reinvestment_rate>*)

USAGE

MIRR() calculates the modified internal rate of return—that is, the effective interest rate—for a series of irregular cash flows. Enter *<cash_flows>* as an array or cell reference, containing the cash flow amounts. Use cash flow conventions to determine the sign of the dollar values. Cash received is positive and cash paid out is negative. Blank, logical, or text values in this array will be ignored. The *<finance_rate>* is the interest rate that is paid to borrow the investment capital, or the interest that it could have achieved on another investment. The *<reinvestment_rate>* is the rate at which the capital returned from the investment can be reinvested. For both rates, use the fractional value or postfix the percentage with the percent operator.

SEE ALSO

FV(), IPMT(), IRR(), NPER(), NPV(), PMT(), PPMT(), PV()

MMULT()

v: **1.5**

SYNTAX

MMULT(*<array_1>***,***<array_2>***)**

USAGE

MMULT() multiplies two matrices. Since MMULT() returns a matrix, you must select an array of cells with the same number of rows as *<array_1>* and the same number of columns as *<array_2>*, and insert the function into all of the selection by holding down the Command key when pressing

Enter or clicking the check mark. If either matrix contains blank cells, cells containing strings, or cells containing logical values, or if *<array1>* does not have the same number of columns as *<array2>* has rows, the function will return the error value #VALUE!.

SEE ALSO

MDETERM(), MINVERSE(), TRANSPOSE()

MOD()

v: **ALL**

SYNTAX

MOD(*<number>*,*<divisor>***)**

USAGE

MOD() returns the remainder, or modulus, of a division operation for positive values of *<number>*. The result will have the same sign as *<divisor>*. For negative values of *<number>*, the results are largely useless. It is defined as *<number>*–INT(*<number*/*<divisor>*)**<divisor>*, which can be a problem because of the way the INT() function converts negative numbers. To calculate a modulus function that works correctly for both positive and negative numbers, use the relation *<number>*–TRUNC(*<number>*/*<divisor>*)**<divisor>* instead of the MOD() function.

SEE ALSO

INT(), ROUND(), TRUNC(), VALUE()

MONTH()

v: **ALL**

SYNTAX

MONTH(<*serial_day_number*>**)**

USAGE

MONTH() calculates the month of the year that corresponds to a <*serial_day_number*>. This function is not needed to display complete dates, because Excel will automatically convert a <*serial_day_number*> into a date if you format the cell as a date. Use this function where you need the number of the month of the year. MONTH() will ignore any fractional parts (time of day) of a <*serial_day_number*>. See the Introduction for more information about dates and times.

SEE ALSO

DATE(), DATEVALUE(), DAY(), HOUR(), MINUTE(), NOW(), SECOND(), TIME(), TIMEVALUE(), WEEKDAY(), YEAR()

N()

v: 1.5

SYNTAX

N(<*value*>)

USAGE

N() tests a cell for numbers and then returns a number that describes the cell's contents. The function will always return a number, no matter what the contents of <*value*>. If <*value*> is a reference to an array of cells, N() will evaluate only the cell in the upper-left corner of that array, even if it is entered into an array of cells with the Command key held down.

<*value*>	**N(<*value*>)**
a number	the same number
a date in one of the built-in formats	serial_day_number
a logical	1 for TRUE, 0 for FALSE
a string or anything else	0

SEE ALSO

T(), TYPE()

NA()

v: **ALL**

SYNTAX

NA()

USAGE

NA() returns the error value #N/A, which means "not available." It is used as a place-holder for values or formulas you do not have yet. Inserting it wherever the missing data will go, instead of leaving the cells blank, forces any cells that depend on that data to also have the value #N/A. This way, you will not use the results of calculations on invalid data if you forget to insert one of the values or formulas later.

SEE ALSO

ISNA()

NOT()

v: **ALL**

SYNTAX

NOT(<*logical*>)

USAGE

NOT() returns TRUE if the argument is FALSE, or FALSE if it is TRUE.

SEE ALSO

AND(), OR()

NOW()

v: **ALL**

SYNTAX

NOW()

USAGE

NOW() returns the <*serial_day_number*> for the current date and time, as set by the system calendar/clock.

SEE ALSO

DATE(), DATEVALUE(), DAY(), HOUR(), MINUTE(), MONTH(), SECOND(), TIME(), TIMEVALUE(), WEEKDAY(), YEAR()

NPER()

v: **ALL**

SYNTAX

NPER(<*rate*>**,**<*payment*>**,**<*present_value*>**,**
[<*future_value*>],[<*type*>]**)**

USAGE

NPER() calculates the number of periods in an annuity, given its initial or <*present_value*>, its <*future_value*>, the <*payment*> per period, and the interest <*rate*>. The interest rate must be the fractional interest rate per period, or the percent interest rate postfixed with the % operator. If the <*future_value*> is omitted, 0 is assumed. The <*type*> of annuity is 0 (the default; payments made at the end of each period), or 1 (payments at the beginning of each period). Use cash-flow conventions to determine the sign of the dollar values. Cash received is positive, and cash paid out is negative. See **FV()** for more information about annuities and the arguments.

SEE ALSO

FV(), IPMT(), IRR(), MIRR(), NPV(), PMT(), PPMT(), PV(), RATE()

NPV()

v: **ALL**

SYNTAX

NPV(<*rate*>,<*cash_flows1*>[,<*cash_flows2*>,[...]]**)**

USAGE

NPV() calculates the net present value of a series of irregular cash flows. This value is the amount of cash you would have to have now, invested at <*rate*> interest, to generate cash flows in the future that are equivalent to the <*cash_flows*>. The interest <*rate*> is expressed as the fractional rate (not percent) per period. <*cash_flows*> represents one or more cash flows as individual numbers or arrays of numbers. Use cash flow conventions to determine the sign of the dollar values. Cash received is positive and cash paid out is negative. The net present value is calculated with

$$\text{NPV} = \sum_{i=1}^{n} \frac{cash\,flows_i}{(1 + rate)^i}$$

While the cash flows are of irregular size, they are assumed to occur at regular intervals, with the first cash flow at the end of the first period. If the first cash flow occurs at the beginning of the first period, calculate the NPV() of the remaining cash flows, and then add the first cash flow to the result.

SEE ALSO

FV(), IPMT(), IRR(), MIRR(), NPER(), PMT(), PPMT(), PV(), RATE()

OR()

v: **ALL**

SYNTAX

OR(<*logical_1*>[,<*logical_2*>[,...]]**)**

USAGE

OR() returns the logical "OR" of the arguments in its argument list. If any of the arguments in the argument list have the logical value TRUE, OR() returns TRUE. If all of the arguments are FALSE, OR() returns FALSE.

OR() also responds to numbers. A value of 0 is equivalent to FALSE, while any nonzero value is equivalent to TRUE.

SEE ALSO

AND(), NOT()

PI()

v: **ALL**

SYNTAX

PI()

USAGE

PI() returns the numeric value of π. Use it in trigonometric formulas. To convert degrees to radians for the trigonometric functions, SIN(), COS(), and TAN(), use the expression *<degrees>**PI()/180 = *<radians>*.

SEE ALSO

ACOS(), ASIN(), ATAN(), ATAN2(), COS(), SIN(), TAN()

PMT()

v: **ALL**

SYNTAX

PMT(*<rate>***,***<periods>***,***<present_value>***,**
[*<future_value>*],[*<type>*]**)**

USAGE

PMT() calculates the periodic payment of an annuity, given its initial or <*present_value*>, its <*future_value*>, the number of periodic payments (<*periods*>), and the interest <*rate*>. The interest rate must be the fractional interest rate per period, or the percent interest rate postfixed with the % operator. If the <*future_value*> is omitted, 0 is assumed. The <*type*> of annuity is 0 (the default; payments made at the end of each period), or 1 (payments at the beginning of each period). Use cash-flow conventions to determine the sign of the dollar values. Cash received is positive, and cash paid out is negative. See **FV()** for more information about annuities and the arguments.

SEE ALSO

FV(), IPMT(), IRR(), MIRR(), NPER(), NPV(), PPMT(), PV(), RATE()

PPMT()

v: **1.5**

SYNTAX

PPMT(<*rate*>**,**<*period*>**,**<*periods*>**,**<*present_value*>**,**
[<*future_value*>],[<*type*>]**)**

USAGE

PPMT() calculates the part of a periodic payment of an annuity that is principle, as opposed to the part that is interest (see **IPMT()**), at some point during the lifetime of the annuity.

PPMT() calculates the principle, given its initial or *<present_value>*, its *<future_value>*, the number of periodic payments (*<periods>*), the interest *<rate>*, and the *<period>* at which to calculate the principle. The interest rate must be the fractional interest rate per period, or the percent interest rate postfixed with the % operator. If the *<future_value>* is omitted, 0 is assumed. The *<type>* of annuity is 0 (the default; payments made at the end of each period), or 1 (payments at the beginning of each period). Use cash-flow conventions to determine the sign of the dollar values. Cash received is positive, and cash paid out is negative. See **FV()** for more information about annuities and the arguments.

PPMT() calculates the future value of a partially paid annuity, multiplies that by the interest rate, and then subtracts that product from the payment to get the principle payment.

SEE ALSO

FV(), IPMT(), IRR(), MIRR(), NPER(), NPV(), PMT(), PV(), RATE()

PRODUCT()

v: **1.5**

SYNTAX

PRODUCT(<*values_1*>[,<*values_2*>[,...]])

USAGE

PRODUCT() multiplies all of the numbers in its arguments together. Any referenced cells that are blank, or that contain logical values or text, will be ignored. This feature allows your cell reference to include blank lines and column headings without including them in the product. There can be up to 14 arguments, any of which can be be a reference to many cells.

SEE ALSO

AVERAGE(), COUNT(), DPRODUCT(), MAX(), MIN(), STDEV(), SUM(), VAR()

PROPER()

v: **1.5**

SYNTAX

PROPER(<*string*>)

USAGE

PROPER() returns <*string*> with the first character and every character that appears after a nonalphabetic character capitalized. All other characters are converted to lowercase.

SEE ALSO

LOWER(), UPPER()

PV()

v: ALL

SYNTAX

PV(<*rate*>**,**<*periods*>**,**<*payment*>**,[**<*future_value*>**],**
[<*type*>**])**

USAGE

PV() calculates the present value of an annuity, the amount of cash you would have to put in an interest-bearing account now for it to be equivalent to an annuity with the given number of periods and payments. PV() calculates the present value, given its <*future_value*>, the number of periodic payments (<*periods*>), the <*payment*> per period, and the interest <*rate*>. The interest rate must be the fractional interest rate per period, or the percent interest rate postfixed with the % operator. If the <*future_value*> is omitted, 0 is assumed. The <*type*> of annuity is 0 (the default; payments made at the end of each period), or 1 (payments at the beginning of each period). Use cash-flow conventions to determine the sign of the dollar values. Cash received is positive, and cash paid out is negative. See **FV()** for more information about annuities and the arguments.

SEE ALSO

FV(), IPMT(), IRR(), MIRR(), NPER(), NPV(), PMT(), PPMT(), RATE()

RAND()

v: **ALL**

SYNTAX

RAND()

USAGE

RAND() returns a different random number between 0 and 1 each time the worksheet is recalculated. To get a random number in a range other than 0 to 1, multiply RAND() by the difference between the upper and lower limits of the range, and then add the lower limit of the range.

To work with a fixed set of random numbers, copy them with the Edit Copy command and then paste them back with the Edit Paste Special command with the Values Only button checked. You can also fix a random value by selecting the function in the menu bar and executing the Options Calculate Now command. The function will be replaced with its current value.

RATE()

v: **ALL**

SYNTAX

RATE(<*periods*>**,**<*payment*>**,**<*present_value*>**,**
[<*future_value*>],[<*type*>],[<*guess*>]**)**

USAGE

RATE() calculates the effective interest rate of an annuity, the interest rate you would need to earn to receive the same payments as the annuity. The function calculates the interest rate, given its initial or <*present_value*>, its <*future_value*>, the number of periodic payments (<*periods*>), and the <*payment*> per period. The solution is found iteratively, using <*guess*> as a starting point. The closer <*guess*> is to the correct rate, the faster the iteration will converge. Enter <*guess*> as a fractional value or postfix the percentage with a percent operator. If the <*future_value*> is omitted, 0 is assumed. The <*type*> of annuity is 0 (the default; payments made at the end of each period), or 1 (payments at the beginning of each period). Use cash-flow conventions to determine the sign of the dollar values. Cash received is positive, and cash paid out is negative. See **FV()** for more information about annuities and the arguments.

If the iteration process does not converge after 20 iterations, RATE() will return the value #NUM!. If this happens, try a different value for <*guess*>.

SEE ALSO

FV(), IPMT(), IRR(), MIRR(), NPER(), NPV(), PMT(), PPMT(), PV()

REPLACE()

v: **1.5**

SYNTAX

REPLACE(<*old_string*>**,**<*start_character*>**,**<*characters*>**,** <*new_string*>**)**

USAGE

REPLACE() deletes <*characters*> characters from <*old_string*> starting at character number <*start_character*>. The remaining right half of <*old_string*> is then shifted left or right until a sufficient hole exists to insert <*new_string*>. REPLACE() then inserts <*new_string*> at that point and returns the result.

SEE ALSO

CLEAN(), LEFT(), MID(), RIGHT(), SEARCH(), SUBSTITUTE(), TRIM()

REPT()

v: **ALL**

SYNTAX

REPT(<*string*>,<*number_of_times*>**)**

USAGE

Returns a string that consists of <*string*> repeated <*number_of_times*>. This value must be greater than or equal to 0. If it equals 0, the empty or null string ("") will be returned.

RIGHT()

v: **1.5**

SYNTAX

RIGHT(<*string*>[,<*number_of_characters*>]**)**

USAGE

RIGHT() returns a string containing the rightmost <*number_of_characters*> from <*string*>. If <*number_of_characters*> is greater than the length of <*string*>, all of <*string*> is returned. This value must be greater than 0. If it is omitted, 1 is assumed.

SEE ALSO

CLEAN(), LEFT(), MID(), REPLACE(), SEARCH(), SUBSTITUTE(), TRIM()

ROUND()

v: **ALL**

SYNTAX

ROUND(<*number*>**,**<*number_of_digits*>**)**

USAGE

ROUND() returns <*number*> rounded to the nearest number with <*number_of_digits*> digits to the right (or left) of the decimal. Positive values of <*number_of_digits*> round to the right of the decimal; negative values, to the left. If <*number_of_digits*> is 0, the nearest integer is returned. Values of 0.5 or larger in the rounded-off digits are always rounded up; all others are rounded down. For example, if <*number_of_digits*> is 0, 12.5 will round to 13, and –12.5 will round to –13.

SEE ALSO

INT(), MOD(), TRUNC(), VALUE()

ROW()

v: **ALL**

SYNTAX

ROW([<*reference*>]**)**

USAGE

ROW() returns the row number of <*reference*> if the reference is to a single cell or row of cells. If the cell reference contains more than one row, ROW() returns a vertical array of row numbers, one for each row in the cell reference. To get the array output, select a vertical group of cells, large enough to contain the array. Put the ROW() command in the top cell and hold down the Command key when pressing Enter or clicking the check mark. See the Introduction for more information about arrays.

SEE ALSO

ARRAYS, COLUMN()

ROWS()

v: ALL

SYNTAX

ROWS(<*array*>**)**

USAGE

ROW() returns the number of rows in <*array*>. See the Introduction for more information about arrays.

SEE ALSO

COLUMNS()

SEARCH()

v: **ALL**

SYNTAX

SEARCH(<*search_string*>,<*string*>[,<*start_character*>]**)**

USAGE

SEARCH() looks for <*search_string*> in <*string*>, starting at character number <*start_character*>. It then returns the location of the first character of the first occurrence of <*search_string*>. The search is not case sensitive. If <*search_string*> is not found, or if <*start_character*> is 0 or less than 0, SEARCH() returns the error value #VALUE!. If <*start_character*> is omitted, 1 is assumed.

SEE ALSO

CLEAN(), LEFT(), MID(), REPLACE(), RIGHT(), SUBSTITUTE(), TRIM()

SECOND()

v: ALL

SYNTAX

SECOND(*<serial_day_number>*)

USAGE

SECOND() extracts the second from the *<serial_day_number>*. SECOND() is not needed to display a time, because Excel will do this automatically if you format a cell as a time.

The SECOND() function will ignore any integer parts (dates) of a *<serial_day_number>*. See the Introduction for more information on dates and times.

SEE ALSO

DATE(), DAY(), HOUR(), MINUTE(), MONTH(), NOW(), TIME(), WEEKDAY(), YEAR()

SIGN()

v: ALL

SYNTAX

SIGN(*<number>*)

USAGE

SIGN() returns the number 1 with the sign of <*number*>. It is equivalent to <*number*>/ABS(<*number*>).

SEE ALSO

ABS()

SIN()

***v*: ALL**

SYNTAX

SIN(<*angle*>**)**

USAGE

SIN() calculates the sine of <*angle*>, which must be expressed in radians. The result is in the range –1 to 1. If your angle is in degrees, multiply it by PI()/180 to convert it into radians.

SEE ALSO

ACOS(), ASIN(), ATAN(), ATAN2(), COS(), PI(), TAN()

SLN()

v: **1.5**

SYNTAX

SLN(<*cost*>**,**<*salvage_value*>**,**<*life*>**)**

USAGE

SLN() calculates the depreciation on an asset using the straight-line method. The straight-line method is the simplest of the depreciation methods, depreciating an equal amount of an asset's value every period. It uses the equation (<*cost*>–<*salvage_value*>)/<*life*>, where <*cost*> is the original cost of the asset, <*salvage_value*> is the value of an asset at the end of its lifetime, and <*life*> is the lifetime of the asset in periods.

SEE ALSO

DDB(), SYD()

SQRT()

v: **ALL**

SYNTAX

SQRT(<*number*>**)**

USAGE

The SQRT() function returns the square root of <*number*>. The number must not be less than 0.

STDEV() and STDEVP()

v: STDEV() all; STDEVP() 1.5

SYNTAX

STDEV(<*values_1*>[,<*values_2*>[,...]])
STDEVP(<*values_1*>[,<*values_2*>[,...]])

USAGE

STDEV() calculates the sample standard deviation of <*values1*>, <*values2*>, ..., one or more lists of numbers. If there are blank cells, or cells containing strings or logical values in a cell reference, they will not be included in the calculation.

The sample standard deviation is calculated with the following equation:

$$S_y = \sqrt{\frac{\sum_{i=1}^{n}(y_i - <y>)^2}{n-1}}$$

where S_y is the sample standard deviation, the y_i are the data values, $<y>$ is the average of the data values, and n is the number of data values. The sample variance $((S_y)^2 = \text{VAR}())$ is equal to the square of this equation.

The STDEVP() function works in the same way as the STDEV() function, except that it calculates the true population standard deviation.

$$\sigma_y = \sqrt{\frac{\sum_{i=1}^{n} (y_i - \langle y \rangle)^2}{n}}$$

The population variance ($(\sigma_y)^2$ = VARP()) is equal to the square of this equation.

The sample standard deviation is used to estimate the standard deviation of a whole population using only a sample of that population. In most situations, you will only be working with a sample of a population, so the sample standard deviation is the correct function to use. The true population standard deviation is used when you have a whole population to work with rather than just a sample of a population. The true population standard deviation is also known as the biased estimate of the standard deviation.

SEE ALSO

AVERAGE(), COUNT(), DSTDEV(), DSTDEVP(), MAX(), MIN(), PRODUCT(), SUM(), VAR(), VARP()

SUBSTITUTE()

v: 1.5

SYNTAX

SUBSTITUTE(<*target_string*>**,**<*old_string*>**,**<*new_string*> [**,**<*instance*>]**)**

USAGE

SUBSTITUTE() returns a string with every occurence of <*old_string*> in <*target_string*> replaced with <*new_string*>. The lengths of <*old_string*> and <*new_string*> do not need to be the same; the function will adjust the resulting string for any differences. If the integer <*instance*> is specified, only that one instance of the <*old_string*> will be replaced. SUBSTITUTE() makes only a single pass on <*target_string*>, so instances of <*old_string*> in <*new_string*> will not be substituted for.

SEE ALSO

CLEAN(), LEFT(), MID(), RIGHT(), REPLACE(), SEARCH(), TRIM()

SUM()

v: ALL

SYNTAX

SUM(<*values_1*>[,<*values_2*>[,...]]**)**

USAGE

SUM() adds up all the numbers in the arguments. Any referenced cells that are blank or contain logical values or text will be ignored. You can thus include blank lines and column headings in a cell reference without including them in the sum. There can be up to 14 arguments, any of which can be a reference to many cells.

SEE ALSO

AVERAGE(), COUNT(), DSUM(), MAX(), MIN(), PRODUCT(), STDEV(), VAR(), VARP()

SYD()

v: 1.5

SYNTAX

SYD(<*cost*>,<*salvage_value*>,<*life*>,<*current_period*>**)**

USAGE

The SYD() function calculates the depreciation on an asset at a specific period in its lifetime, using the sum-of-the-years'-digits method. This accelerated method calculates depreciation by first summing the digits, 1, 2, 3, 4, ... <*life*>. Then, the depreciation at the <*current_period*> is

$$\text{SYD()} = \left(\frac{(cost\ -\ salvage\ value)(life\ -\ current\ period\ +1)}{(1+2+3+\ldots life)} \right)$$

where <*cost*> is the original cost of the asset, <*salvage_value*> is the value of the asset at the end of its lifetime, <*life*> is the lifetime of the asset in periods, and <*current_period*> is the period at which you want the depreciation calculated.

Note that <*life*> and <*current_period*> must be in the same units (months, years, and so forth).

SEE ALSO

DDB(), SLN()

T()

v: 1.5

SYNTAX

T(<*value*>)

USAGE

The T() function tests a cell for a string and returns a string describing the cell's contents. If <*value*> is an array, T() will test only the cell in the upper-left corner. Use it for error trapping, to prevent calculations between strings and numbers. It is included primarily for compatibility with other spreadsheets, as Excel will concatenate a number and a string with the & operator without causing an error. It will convert the number to a string before concatenating it to another string. The T() function, however, will not convert a number to a string, but will use the empty or null string instead.

<*value*>	**T(<*value*>)**
a string	the same string
anything else	the null string ("")

SEE ALSO

N(), TYPE()

TAN()

v: **ALL**

SYNTAX

TAN(<*angle*>**)**

USAGE

TAN() calculates the tangent of <*angle*>, which must be expressed in radians. If your angle is in degrees, multiply it by PI()/180.

SEE ALSO

ACOS(), ASIN(), ATAN(), ATAN2(), COS(), PI(), SIN()

TEXT()

v: **ALL**

SYNTAX

TEXT(<*number*>**,**<*format*>**)**

USAGE

TEXT() converts a number to a text string according to <*format*>. The format can be any of those in the Format Number command, except for the General format (see the FORMAT.NUMBER() macro function). It can also be any custom format that follows the rules of the Format Number command. It will not follow the color formats, but will be displayed in the text color defined for the cell that contains it.

SEE ALSO

DOLLAR(), FIXED(), ROUND(), VALUE()

TIME() and TIMEVALUE()

***v:* TIME() ALL; TIMEVALUE() 1.5**

SYNTAX

TIME(<*hour*>**,**<*minute*>**,**<*second*>**)**
TIMEVALUE(<*time_string*>**)**

USAGE

The TIME() function converts the integers <*hour*>, <*minute*> and <*second*> into a <*serial_day_number*>. Values for <*hour*> greater than 24 will be converted modulo 24. That is, 26 will become 2, and so forth.

The TIMEVALUE() function converts the string representation of a time in <*time_string*> into a <*serial_day_number*>. TIMEVALUE() can be used to extract the date from a string that contains a date and a time.

These functions are not often needed, because Excel will automatically convert text you type in date format into a *<serial_day_number>*. Use the TIME() function where the hour, minute, and second are in separate cells, or are the result of formulas. If the time is part of a formula, you can either use the TIME() or TIMEVALUE() functions, or just put the time (in standard time format) in quotes. See the FORMAT.NUMBER() macro function for the time formats. See the Introduction for more information on dates and times.

SEE ALSO

DAY(), DATE(), DATEVALUE(), HOUR(), MINUTE(), MONTH(), NOW(), SECOND(), WEEKDAY(), YEAR()

TRANSPOSE()

***v:* ALL**

SYNTAX

TRANSPOSE(*<array>*)

USAGE

TRANSPOSE() returns the transpose of a matrix. Since the TRANSPOSE() function returns a matrix, you must select an array of cells with the same number of rows as *<array>* has columns and the same number of columns as *<array>* has rows, and then insert the function into all of the selection by holding down the Command key when pressing Enter or clicking the check mark. The transpose of a matrix is a matrix with the rows and columns exchanged. The transpose of a vertical vector is a horizontal vector. Note that the cell reference can consist of only one area (see **AREAS()**).

SEE ALSO

MDETERM(), MINVERSE(), MMULT()

TREND()

v: **ALL**

SYNTAX

TREND(<*array_y*>**,**<*array_x*>**,[**<*array_x2*>**])**

USAGE

TREND() uses linear regression to fit a linear curve ($y = m*x + b$) to the <*array_x*> and <*array_y*> data. The <*array_x2*> argument is an array or cell reference containing *x* data for calculating a new set of *y* data using the curve fit. The linear curve fit is calculated in the same manner as for the LINEST() function. The <*array_x2*> data, or the <*array_x*> data if <*array_x2*> is omitted, is then inserted into the linear equation and a new array of *y* data is returned. This function returns an array the same size as <*array_x2*> or <*array_x*>, so you must select an area on the worksheet of the appropriate size, and insert the function into all of the cells by holding down the Command key when pressing Enter or clicking the check mark.

The *<array_x>* and *<array_y>* arrays must be the same size, because the values in these arrays are assumed to correspond one for one. If *<array_x>* is omitted, the numbers 1, 2, 3, ... are assumed.

SEE ALSO

GROWTH(), LINEST(), LOGEST()

TRIM()

v: **1.5**

SYNTAX

TRIM(*<string>*)

USAGE

TRIM() returns *<string>* with any leading and trailing spaces removed, and any multiple internal spaces reduced to single spaces.

SEE ALSO

CLEAN(), LEFT(), MID(), RIGHT(), REPLACE(), SEARCH(), SUBSTITUTE(), TRIM()

TRUE()

v: **ALL**

SYNTAX

TRUE()

USAGE

TRUE() returns the logical value TRUE. You do not need to use this function to get the value TRUE. Simply type the word TRUE where it is needed, and Excel will interpret it as the logical value rather than a text string. To place a text string rather than the logical value in a cell, put it in quotes.

SEE ALSO

FALSE()

TRUNC()

v: **1.5**

SYNTAX

TRUNC(<*number*>**)**

USAGE

TRUNC() returns the integer part of <*number*> by simply truncating the fractional part. To get the fractional part, use the expression <*number*>–TRUNC(<*number*>). The result will have the same sign as <*number*>.

SEE ALSO

INT(), MOD(), ROUND()

TYPE()

v: **ALL**

SYNTAX

TYPE(<*value*>**)**

USAGE

The TYPE() function tests the contents of its argument and returns a numeric code that describes the contents. The function always returns a number, no matter what the contents of <*value*>. Use it to determine the type of a cell's contents before trying to manipulate them.

<*value*>	**TYPE(<*value*>)**
a number	1
a date (in one of the built-in formats)	1
a string	2

<value>	**TYPE(*<value>*)**
a logical	14
an error value	16
an array	64

If *array_1* has been defined as {1,2;3,4} with the Formula Define Name command (see the DEFINE.NAME() macro function), **=TYPE(array_1)** will return the number 1 rather than the expected 64. Also, **=TYPE(C1:C2)** returns the number 16, indicating an error, rather than the expected 64. However, if you enter **=TYPE(C1:C2)** as an array into two vertical cells while holding down the Command key, or enter **=TYPE(array_1)** into a two-by-two array while holding down the Command key, you will get the expected number 64 in all of the cells. I would not depend on these "features" to be in future releases of Excel.

SEE ALSO

N(), T()

UPPER()

v: **1.5**

SYNTAX

UPPER(<*string*>**)**

USAGE

UPPER() returns <*string*> with all characters converted to upper case.

SEE ALSO

LOWER(), PROPER()

VALUE()

v: **ALL**

SYNTAX

VALUE(<*string*>)

USAGE

VALUE() converts a string representation of a number into a number, or a date or time into a *serial day number*. The numbers, dates and times must be in one of the built-in formats (see the **FORMAT.NUMBER()** macro function).

You should never need this function, because Excel will automatically convert string representations of dates or numbers into numbers in formulas. If a cell contains only a cell reference to a string that contains a number, Excel will leave it a string, because a number is not needed. In this case, you can use this function to force interpretation as a number.

SEE ALSO

DOLLAR(), FIXED(), ROUND(), TEXT()

VAR() and VARP()

v: **VAR() all; VARP() 1.5**

SYNTAX

VAR(<*values_1*>[,<*values_2*>[,...]])
VARP(<*values_1*>[,<*values_2*>[,...]])

USAGE

The VAR() function calculates the sample variance of a list of numbers. Blank cells and those containing strings or logical values in a cell reference are not included in the calculation. The sample variance is the square of the sample standard deviation. See **STD()** for the equation used to calculate that value.

The VARP() function works in the same way as the VAR() function, except that it calculates the true population variance. This value is the square of the true population standard deviance. See **STD()** for the equation used.

The sample variance is used to estimate the variance of a whole population using only a sample of that population. In most situations, you will only be working with a sample of a population, so the sample variance is the correct function to use. The true population variance is used when you have a whole population.

SEE ALSO

AVERAGE(), COUNT(), DVAR(), DVARP(), MAX(), MIN(), PRODUCT(), STDEV(), STDEVP(), SUM()

VLOOKUP()

v: **ALL**

SYNTAX

VLOOKUP(*<lookup_value>***,***<search_array>***,** *<column_index>***)**

USAGE

VLOOKUP() searches the first column of *<search_array>* top to bottom for the largest value that is less than or equal to *<lookup_value>*. It then moves across to the column specified by *<column_index>*, and returns the contents of the cell found there. The contents of the first column can be either values or text, and must be in ascending order, with numbers < text < logicals. If *<column_index>* is less than 1, the error value #VALUE! will be returned. If *<column_index>* is 1, the contents of the cell in the first column will be returned. If *<column_index>* is greater than the number of columns in *<search_array>*, the function will return the error value #REF!. If *<lookup_value>* is less than the first value in the first column, the function will return the error value #N/A.

SEE ALSO

HLOOKUP(), INDEX(), LOOKUP(), MATCH()

WEEKDAY()

v: **ALL**

SYNTAX

WEEKDAY(*<serial_day_number>*)

USAGE

WEEKDAY() calculates the day of the week that corresponds to a *<serial_day_number>*. The function returns an integer from 1 to 7, where 1 is Sunday and 7 is Saturday.

The function ignores any fractional parts (time of day) of a *<serial_day_number>*. See the Introduction for more information on dates and times.

SEE ALSO

DATE(), DATEVALUE(), DAY(), HOUR(), MINUTE(), MONTH(), NOW(), SECOND(), TIME(), TIMEVALUE(), WEEKDAY()

YEAR()

v: **ALL**

SYNTAX

YEAR(<*serial_day_number*>**)**

USAGE

YEAR() returns the numeric value of the year that corresponds to a <*serial_day_number*>.

This function is not needed to display complete dates, because Excel automatically converts a <*serial_day_number*> into a day if you format the cell as a date. Use this function where you need the number of the year.

The function ignores any fractional parts (time of day) of a <*serial_day_number*>. See the Introduction for more information on dates and times.

SEE ALSO

DATE(), DATEVALUE(), DAY(), HOUR(), MINUTE(), MONTH(), NOW(), SECOND(), TIME(), TIMEVALUE(), WEEKDAY()

Selections from The SYBEX Library

APPLE/MACINTOSH

Mastering ProDOS
Timothy Rice/Karen Rice
260pp. Ref. 315-5
An in-depth look at the inner workings of ProDOS, for advanced users and programmers – with discussion of system programming techniques, sample programs in BASIC and assembler, and scores of ready-made ProDOS utility routines.

Mastering Adobe Illustrator
David A. Holzgang
330pp. Ref. 463-1
This text provides a complete introduction to Adobe Illustrator, bringing new sophistication to artists using computer-aided graphics and page design technology. Includes a look at PostScript, the page composition language used by Illustrator.

Desktop Publishing with Microsoft WORD On the Macintosh
Tim Erickson/William Finzer
517pp. Ref. 447-X
The authors have woven a murder mystery through the text, using the sample publications as clues. Explanations of page layout, headings, fonts and styles, columnar text, and graphics are interwoven with the mystery theme of this exciting teaching method.

Mastering WordPerfect on the Macintosh
Kay Yarborough Nelson
462pp. Ref. 515-8
The graphics-oriented Macintosh version of WordPerfect is discussed from startup to mastery in this excellent tutorial. Detailed treatment of software features, plus sample layouts and design tips especially for the Mac. Includes Fast Track speed notes.

Understanding HyperCard
Greg Harvey
580pp. Ref. 506-9
The enormous potential of this major software development is clarified and explained in this extensive hands-on tutorial which covers all aspects of the HyperCard and HyperText world, using step-by-step discussions, examples, and insights. The best way to construct, fill, and use stacks efficiently is covered in detail.

HyperTalk Instant Reference
Greg Harvey
316pp. Ref. 530-1
For serious HyperCard users, this fingertip reference offers complete, cross-referenced summaries of HyperTalk commands, functions, properties, and constants. Examples of usage and an introduction to Scripting are provided.

Mastering AppleWorks (Second Edition)
Elna Tymes
479pp. Ref. 398-8
New chapters on business applications, data sharing DIF and Applesoft BASIC make this practical, in-depth tutorial even better. Full details on AppleWorks desktop, word processing, spreadsheet and database functions.

AppleWorks Tips and Techniques (Second Edition)
Robert Ericson
462pp. Ref. 480-1
An indispensible collection of timesaving techniques, practical solutions, and tips on undocumented problems for every AppleWorks user. This expanded new edition covers all versions through 2.0, and includes in-depth treatment of macros.

The ABC's of Excel on the Macintosh

Douglas Hergert

314pp. Ref. 562-X

This title is written for users who want a quick way to get started with this highly-acclaimed spreadsheet program. The ABC's offers a rich collection of hands-on examples and step-by-step instructions for working with worksheets, charts, databases, and macros. Covers Excel through Version 1.5.

Mastering Excel on the Macintosh (Second Edition)

Carl Townsend

607pp. Ref. 439-9

A new edition of our popular hands-on guide to using Excel's extensive worksheet, database, and graphics capabilities. With in-depth coverage of special features and techniques, sample applications, and detailed treatment of macros.

Programming the Macintosh in Assembly Language

Steve Williams

779pp. Ref. 263-9

A comprehensive tutorial and reference covering assembly-language basics, the 68000 architecture and instruction set, the Macintosh Toolbox, linking with high-level languages and more; plus an extensive macro library and sample programs.

Programming the Macintosh in C

Bryan J. Cummings/Lawrence J. Pollack

294pp. Ref. 328-7

A comprehensive introduction to C programming, especially for Macintosh users. Covers the design philosophy and special advantages of C, as well as every feature of the language. With extensive reference material.

SPREADSHEETS AND INTEGRATED SOFTWARE

The ABC's of 1-2-3 (Second Edition)

Chris Gilbert/Laurie Williams

245pp. Ref. 355-4

Online Today recommends it as "an easy and comfortable way to get started with the program." An essential tutorial for novices, it will remain on your desk as a valuable source of ongoing reference and support. For Release 2.

Mastering 1-2-3 (Second Edition)

Carolyn Jorgensen

702pp. Ref. 528-X

Get the most from 1-2-3 Release 2 with this step-by-step guide emphasizing advanced features and practical uses. Topics include data sharing, macros, spreadsheet security, expanded memory, and graphics enhancements.

Lotus 1-2-3 Desktop Companion (SYBEX Ready Reference Series)

Greg Harvey

976pp. Ref. 501-8

A full-time consultant, right on your desk. Hundreds of self-contained entries cover every 1-2-3 feature, organized by topic, indexed and cross-referenced, and supplemented by tips, macros and working examples. For Release 2.

Advanced Techniques in Lotus 1-2-3

Peter Antoniak/E. Michael Lunsford

367pp. Ref. 556-5

This guide for experienced users focuses on advanced functions, and techniques for designing menu-driven applications using macros and the Release 2 command language. Interfacing techniques and add-on products are also considered.

Lotus 1-2-3 Tips and Tricks

Gene Weisskopf

396pp. Ref. 454-2

A rare collection of timesavers and tricks for longtime Lotus users. Topics include macros, range names, spreadsheet design, hardware considerations, DOS operations, efficient data analysis, printing, data interchange, applications development, and more.

Lotus 1-2-3 Instant Reference SYBEX Prompter Series
Greg Harvey/Kay Yarborough Nelson
296pp. Ref. 475-5; 4 3/4x8
Organized information at a glance. When you don't have time to hunt through hundreds of pages of manuals, turn here for a quick reminder: the right key sequence, a brief explanation of a command, or the correct syntax for a specialized function.

Mastering Lotus HAL
Mary V. Campbell
342pp. Ref. 422-4
A complete guide to using HAL "natural language" requests to communicate with 1-2-3—for new and experienced users. Covers all the basics, plus advanced HAL features such as worksheet linking and auditing, macro recording, and more.

Mastering Symphony (Fourth Edition)
Douglas Cobb
857pp. Ref. 494-1
Thoroughly revised to cover all aspects of the major upgrade of Symphony Version 2, this Fourth Edition of Doug Cobb's classic is still "the Symphony bible" to this complex but even more powerful package. All the new features are discussed and placed in context with prior versions so that both new and previous users will benefit from Cobb's insights.

The ABC's of Quattro
Alan Simpson/Douglas J. Wolf
286pp. Ref. 560-3
Especially for users new to spreadsheets, this is an introduction to the basic concepts and a guide to instant productivity through editing and using spreadsheet formulas and functions. Includes how to print out graphs and data for presentation. For Quattro 1.1.

Mastering Quattro
Alan Simpson
576pp. Ref. 514-X
This tutorial covers not only all of Quattro's classic spreadsheet features, but also its added capabilities including extended graphing, modifiable menus, and the macro debugging environment. Simpson brings out how to use all of Quattro's new-generation-spreadsheet capabilities.

Mastering Framework II
Douglas Hergert/Jonathan Kamin
509pp. Ref. 390-2
This business-minded tutorial includes a complete introduction to idea processing, "frames," and software integration, along with its comprehensive treatment of word processing, spreadsheet, and database management with Framework.

The ABC's of Excel on the IBM PC
Douglas Hergert
326pp. Ref. 567-0
This book is a brisk and friendly introduction to the most important features of Microsoft Excel for PC's. This beginner's book discusses worksheets, charts, database operations, and macros, all with hands-on examples. Written for all versions through Version 2.

Mastering Excel on the IBM PC
Carl Townsend
628pp. Ref. 403-8
A complete Excel handbook with step-by-step tutorials, sample applications and an extensive reference section. Topics include worksheet fundamentals, formulas and windows, graphics, database techniques, special features, macros and more.

Mastering Enable
Keith D. Bishop
517pp. Ref. 440-2
A comprehensive, practical, hands-on guide to Enable 2.0—integrated word processing, spreadsheet, database management, graphics, and communications—from basic concepts to custom menus, macros and the Enable Procedural Language.

n	ASCII	n	ASCII	n	ASCII	n	ASCII
0		32		64	@	96	`
1	□	33	!	65	A	97	a
2		34	"	66	B	98	b
3		35	#	67	C	99	c
4		36	$	68	D	100	d
5		37	%	69	E	101	e
6	□	38	&	70	F	102	f
7	□	39	'	71	G	103	g
8	□	40	(	72	H	104	h
9		41	)	73	I	105	i
10	□	42	*	74	J	106	j
11	□	43	+	75	K	107	k
12	□	44	,	76	L	108	l
13		45	-	77	M	109	m
14	□	46	.	78	N	110	n
15	□	47	/	79	O	111	o
16	□	48	0	80	P	112	p
17	□	49	1	81	Q	113	q
18	□	50	2	82	R	114	r
19	□	51	3	83	S	115	s
20	□	52	4	84	T	116	t
21	□	53	5	85	U	117	u
22	□	54	6	86	V	118	v
23	□	55	7	87	W	119	w
24	□	56	8	88	X	120	x
25	□	57	9	89	Y	121	y
26	□	58	:	90	Z	122	z
27	□	59	;	91	[	123	{
28	□	60	<	92	\	124	|
29	□	61	=	93	]	125	}
30	□	62	>	94	^	126	~
31	□	63	?	95	_	127	

ASCII codes(n) and characters for Macintosh Geneva font